ART IN
THE PRIMARY
SCHOOL

JOHN LANCASTER

ROUTLEDGE

London and New York

First published 1990
by Routledge
11 New Fetter Lane, London EC4P 4EE

Simultaneously published in the USA and Canada
by Routledge
a division of Routledge, Chapman and Hall, Inc.
29 West 35th Street, New York, NY 10001

© 1990 John Lancaster

Typesetting by Witwell, Southport
Printed in Great Britain by
Richard Clay Ltd, Bungay, Suffolk

British Library Cataloguing in Publication Data
Lancaster, John, *1930–*
   Art in the primary school. – (Subjects in the primary
   school)
   1. Great Britain. Primary schools. Curriculum
   subjects: Arts Teaching
   I. Title   II. Series
   372.5'044'0941
   ISBN 0–415–04242–9

Library of Congress Cataloging in Publication Data

Lancaster, John, 1930–
   Art in the primary school/John Lancaster.
      p.   cm. — (Subjects in the primary school series)
   Includes bibliographical references.
   ISBN 0–415–04242–9 (pbk.)
   1. Art—Study and teaching (Elementary)
   I. Title.   II. Series.
N350.L337   1990   89–39034
                                                 CIP

Contents

Contents

Figures

Plates

Series Editor's Preface

After a decade of declining rolls, the number of children in primary schools is once again rising in most countries in the western world. The rise brings in its train an urgent demand for new teachers and ministries. School authorities and training institutions are turning to university graduates, offering one-year or other shortened courses rather than the conventional three- or four-year training course.

Such students know that they are keenly sought. Not only does the shortened course make them more immediately available to schools, but also their expertise is highly appropriate to the widespread demand for real subject specialism to be available in the primary school curriculum.

But the translation of degree-level study into effective primary teaching is a difficult task – particularly in the short postgraduate course. This series is designed to help students to make the transition more readily. Each volume helps the reader to see the similarities between study at school and university and goes on, with advice, example and explanation, to show how subject knowledge can be structured and presented effectively in a primary school curriculum. Above all, the series aims to help beginning graduate teachers to transmit the enthusiasm that has led them to become specialists to new generations of young people.

John Eggleston

Acknowledgements

In writing this book I have received help and encouragement from a number of sources. My thanks must go, therefore, to the NSEAD (National Society for Education in Art and Design) at Corsham – in particular to John Steers (General Secretary) and to the members of the Working Party who worked with me in the planning of the Society's book on the teaching of art in primary schools (Lancaster 1987), some of whose illustrative material may have spilled over into this one – especially to Ray Haslam, Bob Clement, and Liz Cotton; to Mavis Eccles, former headteacher, for her inspiration and help over a number of years; to Peter Coleman, formerly Director of Education in the County of Avon, who gave me permission to visit schools; to Kate Tambling, John Parry, Margaret Harvey, Sheila Biggs and Stuart Greenwood for helpful photographs taken in their schools; to Mary Brown, former headteacher in Leicestershire, her staff and children in Melton Mowbray, who also gave me valuable assistance; to former students and colleagues at the College of St Paul and Mary, Cheltenham and the University of Bristol; to Professor John Eggleston; to Janet, a recognized authority on early childhood education, for inspiration; to Joan Gaunt, a highly valued mentor; and finally, to our primary children – those aesthetically educated citizens, parents and teachers of tomorrow – to whom I dedicate this small contribution of mine.

John Lancaster

Introduction

This book is for students who are training to be primary teachers and those classroom teachers who lack experience, or who are not greatly skilled, in teaching art. Students on one-year postgraduate teacher education courses have to adapt quickly to more generalized ways of learning that are quite different from their in-depth degree studies, while having to come to terms with a child-centred learning orientation covering curriculum planning, teaching–learning philosophies and classroom strategies as well as the interrelationship of subject areas across the broad primary curriculum. This can be a confusing and daunting task – albeit an exciting and rewarding one – which is given a sense of reality in periods of practical teaching out in the schools.

I shall be attempting, in this book, to provide a general framework within which teachers can plan classroom activities in art of sound pedagogical value. This will be pragmatic with respect to:

- art teaching philosophies and aims
- basic practical 2D and 3D art and design work of relevance to primary school children
- the kinds of materials suitable for such work
- the way art work can be presented through display
- how art can be assessed
- what art experiences children should have had prior to their secondary schooling ('bench marks of achievement')
- the role of art in cross-curricular work
- out-of-school resources
- cultural and art historical studies

Some case-study examples are used in the text and photographs, where relevant, illustrate children's work or show them doing art. In itself a book is obviously no substitute for classroom experience and can only serve as a complementary resource. It might offer a few ideas and suggestions or even provide a few stimuli or thought-provoking philosophies, but the classroom is really the 'open book' in which lively young humans mingle with an exciting eagerness in what, for them and their teacher, is an educational adventure. It is the workshop where children are developing educated minds and articulated skills.

Artists, designers and craftspeople find that 'making' things with materials is always adventurous and this is what sets art aside as an aspect of the academic curriculum. But it doesn't stop there, for art is an activity which can then be carried on by interested adults throughout their lives. The very act of creating two-dimensional visual imagery and three-dimensional objects – things which did not exist before – is tremendously exciting, giving the creator a real sense of achievement and well-being. Of course, other subject specialists might argue that this also applies to their disciplines, just as much as it does to art. I would hope that they would feel as passionate as I do about my own subject and would welcome their arguments.

What I do know from my experience as a teacher and an artist is that the whole realm of art, design and craft is like a banqueting table which provides a nourishing feast – a feast to be savoured, to be enjoyed and to be digested at leisure. It has been said that we are what we eat; if, therefore, we provide a rich aesthetic feast for young children, we will be providing them with the ingredients for a more fulfilling, visually-related aestheticism and an educated cultural intellect which will help them to balance the overall educational provision which it is the responsibility of schools to administer. Children, however must be happy. They must enjoy their learning. As teachers, let us give them respect, while sharing their happiness and pleasure in 'caring' learning environments which throb with visual interest and excitement.

1

Art in the primary school

What do we mean by art, craft, design and appreciation?

Some educationalists look at art, craft, and design as three distinct subjects, and in the past many teachers taught 'art' and then they taught 'craft'. It is questionable as to what they thought of as 'design' – which is a fundamental component of both art and craft – although this aspect is considered today to be some kind of new subject which must be taught as a discrete discipline. In this book I intend to place these three aspects together under the umbrella of 'art' so that it is easier for me to write about and, I trust, easier for my readers to understand. I shall, of course, refer to all three individually from time to time, and the fourth aspect, 'appreciation', will also be discussed.

Let me begin by looking at 'art', 'craft', 'design' and 'appreciation' as four distinct aspects of the subject. Three of these obviously involve the direct use of materials in classroom situations where children participate actively in artistic production, i.e. in the making of art (whether this be in the form of paintings, prints, patterns, models, posters, pottery, or video films). In my opinion, the fourth aspect, appreciation, grows best from the children's experience of doing art work and therefore it, too, can be said to depend upon the manipulation of materials and the knowledge gained through artistic production. This is a disputable concept about which I shall say more shortly; some educationalists would disagree with this idea, insisting that children can be taught how to 'appreciate' art – whether in an historical or modern context – without actually doing it themselves. What is important, however, is that you, the teacher working in school now, will need to consider this problem and resolve it in your own way.

What do we mean by the terms art, craft, design and appreciation? Are they one and the same thing? Are they interrelated? I suggest that they need to be thought about and propose the following definitions as starting points:

1   The term 'art' covers that area of inventiveness with art and craft materials through which self-expressed emotions, ideas and feelings resulting from the visual interpretation of environmental experiences are communicated, while depending upon acquired craftsmanship and artistry.

2   Craft, on the other hand, embraces the acquirement and utilization of manual skills in the manipulation of two- and three-dimensional materials, hand-tools, and/or mechanical equipment. It provides artists, designers and craftspersons with the means of artistry, or what is known quite simply as making art.

3   Artistry depends upon the imaginative or inventive use of knowledgeable and skilful making and designing, and therefore the design aspect is the knowledgeable area in which inventiveness germinates and develops into recognizable artistic form.

Teachers must recognize that these aspects are interdependent. They simply cannot exist in isolation but rely upon good hand, eye, and brain co-ordination; in other words, they spring from an harmonious relationship. Some years ago schoolchildren 'did some art', perhaps a drawing or a painting, and then they 'did some craft' – perhaps making a raffia mat. If they had an interested teacher they might then do 'some design work' – which might have consisted of making a stencil pattern on the cover of an exercise book. It is important today to ensure that they receive a much broader range of practical experiences in a curriculum which gives them a wider educational grounding.

4   The appreciation aspect tends to be separated from the other aspects. I cannot understand why this is so, unless it stems from teacher uncertainty, for it, too, results best from artistic practice and must be aided by empirical knowledge gained through such experience. It is the thoughtful, critical area in which children make value judgements and assessments of works of art, craft, and design in relation to both their historical and cultural context, and the meaningful place of art in the lives of people world-wide.

As I have already stated, some people – amongst them art critics – seem able to 'appreciate' art without having made it. I would argue that this is not really possible and that their appreciation and criticism cannot be total. Is it possible to appreciate how paint has been laid on a canvas if one has never had the experience of doing it? Can I appreciate the feelings which an astronaut has in stepping on to the moon's surface if I

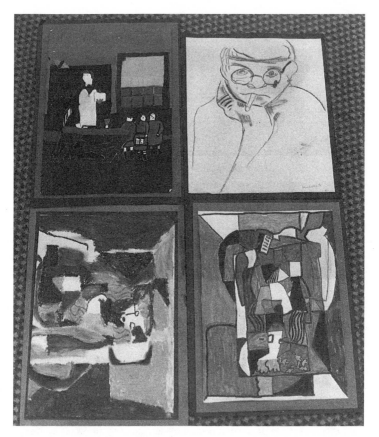

Plate 1   These freely interpreted drawings and paintings by older junior school pupils were copied from reproductions of the works of famous artists. In doing this the children learned a great deal about the artists and how they worked.

have never done this? I fancy not. The Calouste Gulbenkian Foundation Report, *The Arts in Schools* (1982), supports my view, stressing that aesthetic education is important for young children while pointing out that the arts are important in structuring cultural traditions which children with experience as creative communicators will obviously understand better and value more – of course they will, for these will be more meaningful to them.

The 'appreciative' aspect embraces emotional, sensory response by children and the intellectualization of their inventive artistic experiences. It is an area which emphasises the appreciation of artistry, craftsmanship and qualities of design – whether in the cultural artefacts of primitive peoples (and here I include prehistoric examples as shown to us in cave art, as well as the art of native tribes in remote regions of the world today), or in 'fitness for purpose' of, for instance, ergonomically-designed furniture for an office, a home or a spaceship. Its real value lies in promoting critical aesthetic attitudes in children so that they acquire artistic understanding and an appreciation of qualities of beauty while, at the same time, developing sensitivity to works of art and craft and the craft skills used by creative persons.

The role of art in developing children's creativity and aestheticism

Primary teachers have the very interesting task of teaching right across the curriculum, which demands an understanding of how children learn as well as some interest in and knowledge of a variety of subject areas. Most have little knowledge and expertise in art – which embraces designing and making – for they have probably had few opportunities to engage in art activities in their teacher education courses, while earlier their academically-orientated 'O' and 'A' level studies forced many to drop art at secondary level in order they they might concentrate upon 'meaningful' subjects. Yet art and craft (as one subject area) embraces a wide range of practical activities in both two- and three-dimensional aspects, calling for some knowledge on the part of teachers about materials, tools, equipment, storage, the teaching of skills, artistic production, presentation, and assessment; knowledge which is best acquired through involvement and experience over a period of time working in classrooms with children.

When teaching art the teacher is really on a batsman's wicket, for children like doing it. There is a creative urge in every human being – young and old alike – for we all have a natural desire to use our hands and materials as vehicles for artistic expression. If given the right kind of opportunities even pre-school children (some may be only a few months old) will take great delight in expressing themselves with art materials. Place a sheet of paper on the kitchen floor for a three-year-old, and it will grasp a thick crayon firmly and draw linear images crisply and dynamically. Give the same child a hog hair brush and some thick paint

Plate 2   A young, pre-school child will often draw in a vigorous, uninhibited way with pencils or large crayons. This girl is exploring simple 'mark-making', which increases her experience of graphic images and concepts.

and it will relish the experience of painting with an uninhibited confidence which is often quite remarkable to the uninitiated adult. Young children certainly have an inner urge which stimulates creativity, and when they enter school teachers must encourge their 'originator instinct', as Martin Buber (1978) described it, by giving them opportunities to be young artists, craftspersons and designers. This will help them to develop stronger aesthetic sensibilities and an understanding of works of an artistic nature – whether these are of today or of the past – and to train them to develop manipulative skills of value to them in varying curricular aspects and, later, as adults and even as home-owners, in which capacity they will need to be selective in choosing furniture and furnishings, in decorating and in garden planning.

Art, Craft and Design in the Primary School (Lancaster, ed. 1987) stated some basic teaching guidelines for primary teachers. It stressed the sensible planning of art, craft and design curricular and the use of well-prepared and relevant sequentially-structured programmes, and therefore encouraged trainee-teachers, and teachers in schools, to provide for their pupils a realistically-conceived and solid aesthetic education within the broader context of the primary curriculum. Teaching aims and philosophies were discussed, as were ideas on curriculum strategies and support sources, and I shall obviously refer to it from time-to-time.

Basic subjects such as English and mathematics tend to have prime timetable time. I sometimes wonder why. Indeed, I remember studying these and science subjects at school, with art and music thrown in as space-filling activities to which my academically-orientated teachers attached little if any value. Yet I cannot honestly think that the mathematics which I was taught has helped me, since I am hopeless at organizing the household accounts and fail to understand investment procedures and banking – aspects that have real significance to everyday living. School calculations regarding the simultaneous filling and emptying of a bath simply left me bewildered. Who would want to do such a silly thing in the first place? The logic of the event escaped my comprehension and therefore I saw no reason to attempt to understand the problem, let alone work it out. Trigonometry, too, failed to appeal to my more artistically inclined way of thinking, while the squaring of algebraic numbers left me unmoved. I have also had to struggle to learn how to write with a certain degree of fluency, for my School Certificate ('O' level equivalent) course did not give me much direction. When I was in the army on National Service, however, I was responsible for arranging pre-demobilization courses in commerce and industry for officers and other ranks and the letters I composed, and often typed myself, were meaningful and important for the jobs and lives of men and their families. Perhaps this is the difference. When something is 'meaningful' we recognize this and attempt to do it well. If this is so, then what happens in the classroom must be meaningful and children must feel that it is. Art, for me, was different. I liked it and I liked my art master. I went to study it further at art college, very much against parental wishes and teacher advice, and it became a way of life. It was meaningful, it was enjoyable and it was important. I didn't question why it was so, I simply accepted it as such.

Art really is most important in the lives of every individual. We need some artistic and designing expertise and understanding so that we are able to select with confidence well-considered wardrobes of clothes, colour schemes, furniture, furnishings – or simply aesthetically pleasing greeting cards – throughout our lives. We see the products of art every day in advertising, television, magazines, in our streets where street signs and shop window displays catch our attention, in the design of buildings, shopping precincts and parks, as well as in countless other objects which abound in the environment. Our world today is extremely vision-conscious and visual images and aesthetics play powerful roles while exerting a powerful influence on almost everything in it.

If primary teachers intend to provide a well-planned and balanced education for their pupils so that they can go on to enjoy a full and aesthetically-rewarding life then art education must have a valuable place in this. Children are the home-makers, parents and therefore the adult consumers of tomorrow. They are our future citizens and future politicians who will be responsible for environmental projects involving art and design concepts. They will be involved as active decision-makers, possibly tackling large development projects concerned with community life and on quite a vast scale and costing vast amounts of public money. If they have had a sound education in art and design it stands to reason that they will be much more conscious of the value of aesthetics in what they do and will fight for well-considered visual quality in what is conceived. They need, then, to experience and understand the rudiments of aesthetics and design – colour, pattern line, tone, form, structure, arrangement, which are the basic elements of a 'visual grammar'. These elements are the building bricks of art, and in experiencing and using them in making art children will expand their aesthetic understanding not only for their own fulfilment but also for the future good of society. Their lives will be enriched, for they will obtain real pleasure and a sense of personal achievement through producing objects of beauty which others can also enjoy. By developing their pupils' aestheticism, teachers will enable them to create aesthetically-pleasing environments and art objects. This will also give them an increased understanding of the art which others produce or have produced.

The purpose of art in primary education

I have established that art provides children with opportunities to experience 'making' and 'designing', practical experiences in which both inventiveness and direct observational copying are encouraged. It gives many less academically inclined pupils the chance to experience some

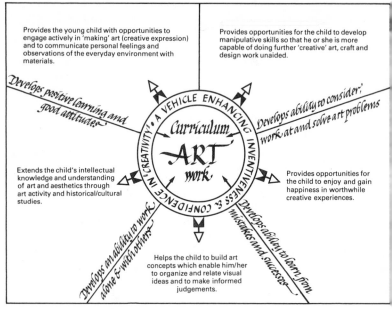

Provides the young child with opportunities to engage actively in 'making' art (creative expression) and to communicate personal feelings and observations of the everyday environment with materials.

Provides opportunities for the child to develop manipulative skills so that he or she is more capable of doing further 'creative' art, craft and design work unaided.

A VEHICLE ENHANCING

Develops positive learning and good attitudes

'CREATIVITY'

Curriculum

ART work.

INVENTIVENESS & CONFIDENCE IN

Develops ability to consider, work at and solve art problems

Extends the child's intellectual knowledge and understanding of art and aesthetics through art activity and historical/cultural studies.

Provides opportunities for the child to enjoy and gain happiness in worthwhile creative experiences.

Develops an ability to work alone & with others

Develops ability to learn from mistakes and successes

Helps the child to build art concepts which enable him/her to organize and relate visual ideas and to make informed judgements.

Figure 1 Chart showing how curriculum art work increases a child's aesthetic understanding and capabilities. (Inspired by HMI criteria, see DES 1987b: 2.)

success. Teachers recognize, of course, that success is very important if learning is to flourish and progress, and if children with learning difficulties in the so-called core subjects can be stimulated by their abilities in doing art work, then this area of curriculum studies can be an invaluable key to the unlocking of other interests and the promoting of learning potential which might otherwise remain stifled or unrealized. Art also offers children with a more academic bent opportunities to enhance their practical knowledge, giving them different intellectual channels of experience which are challenging and rewarding.

Art in the classroom is sometimes misinterpreted as a 'play' activity, but teachers recognize that in the child's terms 'play' is synonymous with 'work'. It involves children in intense concentration and effort, and because the very act of 'playing' is an enjoyable one, they enjoy this effort. It is an activity area which can be a very necessary foil to the more constricting curricular aspects while offering tremendous scope for co-operative working in both large and small groups – in teamwork, where respect for others is engendered and the co-operative sharing of ideas and skills is participated in freely. This is where leadership potential changes, often resulting in the less able children blossoming because their more practically-orientated expertise is required in the production and subsequent realization of intellectual concepts in practical and material terms. In other words, they are given a chance to be successful! It would be wrong to offer the argument that non-academic pupils are skilled practitioners and, conversely, that academic children are not, however. Indeed, this would be a false assumption for time and time again throughout history important artists and craftspeople have been seen to be endowed with a highly-developed intellectualism which complemented their inventive and making skills, raising their artistic products to the highest, most expressive levels.

The visual arts, like those of music, dance, and theatre, are good for the soul and primary school children are fortunate in being able to get right into the essence of art in their humble classrooms. They actually do some art. A few of them might then go on to do a little in their secondary education but how many will ever have the opportunity to be active makers of art again? Will they ever again use art materials? Is the art work which they do at primary school the only such artistic experience they are likely to have? These are questions for primary teachers to bear in mind. They must also ensure that the art which their pupils do is purposeful while also helping to provide a more complete education for them.

On the more mundane side, art is also a 'servicing agency' and it must not be treated as some form of precious aestheticism. It has always had a servicing function in society – whether adult-based or as an aspect of work in schools – and we should continue to see this as an important part of its operation. For instance, drawing and picture-making skills developed in this area will then be applied with more confidence in mathematical and scientific subjects; in the study of costume in history; in the visual presentation of apparatus; in the illustration of poems and passages of prose; and in the production of maps. Puppet theatres will be enhanced by well-conceived and delightfully-made puppets, with colourful and correctly-attributed costumes; by painted backcloths and printed curtains; by painted lettering; and even by carefully-controlled lighting effects. Thoughtful, caring teachers will consider the ramifications carefully and thoroughly. They will plan their general curriculum to be all-embracing and will realize that art must be used to enhance learning potential and to increase excellence across the primary curriculum.

In the early childhood years, particularly those we associate with the pre-school, and infant school stages, a great deal of the art which children do arises from the simple exploration of art materials and the spontaneous pleasure and knowledge derived from those experiences. Children engaged in such explorations should be given numerous opportunities to pursue them in an undirected way, free from adult interference. They can do so with pencils or crayons, with paints and brushes or with modelling and constructional materials, satisfying a

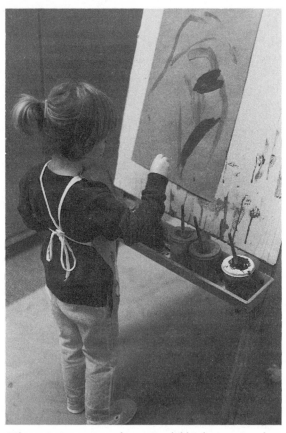

Plate 3 When painting at an easel, a young child is free to mix colours, to use the arm and brush freely as she works, and is able to stand back to see what she has produced on the paper.

natural creative need and, importantly, having the chance to do so repeatedly. This does not mean that the teacher will abandon pupils to a seemingly aimless drift, however, but that the teacher must use his or her professional discretion wisely in order to ensure that children are engaged in worthwhile learning activities. The right kind of activities will encourage them to extend their skills and observations and they will, in consequence, develop questioning attitudes. A lot of art work must be carefully planned and even some 'child-centred' discoveries can be arranged. These will need to be introduced with considerable skill and care, however, to ensure that children engage in educationally worthwhile activities as part of their sequentially-structured learning in school.

I mentioned that children should be free from adult interference. This is an extremely important yet delicate area which requires sensitive action. It is best illustrated by an experience which a newly appointed school inspector had. This person was a graduate who had specialized narrowly in his degree subject at university. He had then taught it in school before obtaining his inspectorial appointment in a large LEA. In his first few months he decided to attend, as a student alongside young teachers, a number of 'specialist' in-service courses which his colleagues were organizing and teaching. It was with some trepidation that he went to an art and craft course for, like many, he had dropped art early in his secondary school years and was somewhat terrified at the prospect of picking up a brush or working in clay. The first day went well. He was told to 'play' with a brush and paint on large sheets of paper, and he found the experience, as he put it 'simply a fun thing to do.' On the second day he went into the pottery workshop and, along with other members of the group, was given some clay. This time, however, he was shown how to make a thumb pot. There was no 'play'. He struggled and made a feeble attempt to do what was demanded. In no time at all he realized that he was hopeless and began to 'play' with some clay, making shapes and small objects with it. The tutor (a fellow 'art' inspector) came along, saw what he was doing and scathingly chided him. 'These are not thumb pots,' he said, 'you are playing about wasting your time.' 'I am indeed playing,' was the retort, 'but certainly not wasting my time for as a potter I am at the five-year-old stage and need to make my own discoveries at my own pace. Thank you very much'. He stalked out of the pottery workshop in a rage and said he would never touch any clay again. What a lesson. I wonder how many times this kind of thing has been done to a child in a classroom by an insensitive teacher? It shows that we need to have a penetrating understanding of the way young children (and also adults) learn, and to permit them to do so in their own way.

As children grow they develop a more critical self-awareness and gradually, particularly at the junior stage, become conscious that their visual expression can lack 'reality'. They have a strong urge to succeed and a desire to be involved in task-oriented project work. It is really at this stage that they begin to search for adult standards of graphicacy – particularly in the drawing and painting of objects and environmental views. This can be sharpened by a concentration on observational copying in which natural or man-made objects are studied intently and drawn precisely.

I wonder just how many primary teachers will have had the experience of selecting a piece of natural form such as a sunflower head, an intricately-formed root or a fern leaf, of placing it on a clean sheet of drawing paper and then – with a 5H pencil, ruler and compass – of making a meticulously studied drawing of it over a period of three days? I fear very few. I, for one, have done this under the stern eye of Victor Pasmore in one of his drawing and painting schools some years ago, and the effect it had on my way of looking, seeing, thinking and graphic representation was tremendous. Think about such a task for a moment. Consider the manipulative skills demanded by the exercise. Note the mathematical and scientific intricacies to be discovered. If children were to make meticulous copies of an insect, a leaf, a metal grid, or whatever in a similar way, it would certainly develop their capacity to think and their drawing skills would be given a sharpness which didn't exist before. They would discover and then represent in graphic terms lines of growth, form, depth, perspective as well as the shapes and divergencies in a piece of natural form affected by climatic changes as it grew: climatic changes which have a dramatic effect upon all living things. This would embrace basic art experiences while adding to their knowledge of science, mathematics and the natural sciences so that they might find themselves moving undirected into a number of areas of study and enquiry smoothly and naturally. Their work could be supported or analysed by written notes and comments, and they could discuss their individual discoveries about natural phenomena, graphic representation (drawing) and visual interpretation. Work of this kind demands a high degree of patience and manual dexterity, while calling for concentrated periods of study, profound effort and disciplined response. How can it be said, then, that art is a time-filling, play activity?

Basic art teaching aims

It is important to be absolutely clear about the fundamental educational aims which underlie the teaching of art, craft and design in the education of primary-age children as, indeed, it is necessary to understand those applicable to every subject. The teacher must be prepared to consider the aims thoughtfully and to state them with assured conviction in planning curricular strategies and lessons. In view of the implementation of the National Curriculum in Britain, and the legal requirements contained in the *Education Reform Act* (1988) as well as the possibility for some schools that governing bodies will take upon themselves much more responsibility for the education of children through the running of schools, it will be important for teachers to be absolutely convinced that what they do is right.

Educationalists have varying opinions as to the specific purpose of art in education, although there is a general consensus as to what is required and what should be taught. How it should be taught varies, for no two teachers can possibly operate in the same way, nor would this be desirable. I conclude, from my own experience in schools, that in teaching art at primary level we should aim to:

1 develop the children's knowledge of materials by allowing them to experiment freely and to encourage them to use materials sensibly in making art
2 ensure that children learn a range of pertinent practical skills so that they develop an expertise in using both materials and equipment correctly
3 provide children with opportunities to express themselves in emotional terms through their art experiences
4 give children opportunities in their art experiences to study and record – by means of thoughtful analytical work – both man-made and natural phenomena
5 involve children in experiencing and learning an artistic visual grammar, partly through points 3 and 4, and also through specific studies in using the elements of art, so that their expertise in the application of visual perception and in communicating visually is increased (A list such as this one will at the very least provide a teacher with a framework for selecting appropriate objectives through which he or she might then go on to achieve them.)
6 involve pupils in project work embracing other areas of the curriculum in which art is an active component

7   provide opportunities for studies of an art historical and cultural
     nature so that children develop appreciation skills associated with
     the examination of works of art and the achievements of artists,
     craftspersons, architects and designers

If we glance at aim number 5 we see that it refers specifically to the
learning of a 'visual grammar' and that this involves experience in, and
knowledge of, what artists call the elements of art. These elements are
the basic and vitally essential components (or what I have sometimes
called the 'building bricks') which form the constituent parts used by
artists, craftspersons and designers in their work – i.e. in producing a
painting, a print, an automobile, a textile pattern, and so on, and
without which no artefact or work of an artistic kind could possibly
exist. In music, the component parts would be the notes, the staves, etc.,
and these would lead to the melodic arrangement of sounds. I list seven
art elements, namely: arrangement; colour; form; line; pattern; shape;
texture; tone.

A brief explanatory sentence or two will help to clarify these:

Arrangement   What I mean by this term is the juxtaposition of two or
    more visual and/or tactile elements into an aesthetically-pleasing
    arrangement. Some artists or teachers would say that 'arrangement'
    means pattern or picture arrangement or what might be called
    'composition'.
Colour   This refers to the quality of light which, in fact, has an effect
    upon human emotions. There are three 'primary' colours – red,
    yellow and blue. 'Secondary' colours consist of orange, green and
    violet – and these result from the mixing of primary colours.
Form   This is really 'shape' and is manifested in three-dimensional
    objects such as those produced in sculpture, pottery, weaving,
    puppetry, craft, design, and technology (CDT), etc., and can be
    experienced simply, so that children understand it, by the inter-
    weaving of the fingers of the left and right hands.
Line   A line may be considered as a long, narrow mark or extended
    point. It may be produced by drawing implements such as a pencil or
    pen and is used in an artistic sense to delineate objects in graphic
    representation, i.e. in drawing. It is also the fundamental basis of
    lettering.
Pattern   A pattern consists of a considered arrangement of shapes,
    forms, textures and colours.

Shape This is a defined area upon a two-dimensional surface – i.e. on paper, card, wood, plastic, canvas, television monitor, etc.

Texture This is simply surface quality and can be seen on both two- and three-dimensional surfaces in the form of small marks and colours. It may be smooth or rough.

Tone This comprises tonal contrasts of lightness and darkness.

If as teachers we are aware of these elements, then we can make a determined effort to see that our pupils experience them when they are doing art in school. Sometimes it will be necessary to plan specific exercises embracing one element only to ensure that children do experience it, think about it, use it and are aware of it in the work of others. At other times an art experience should incorporate more than one element so that the pupils become conversant with them and apply them confidently and with understanding in their artistic endeavours.

2

The framework for planning art activities

The planning of suitable art activities in the primary school context

Primary classrooms are often far from ideal places in which art activities may be initiated, especially as we normally associate the practising of all forms of artistic work with studios and workshops in which materials and special facilities contribute to a creative atmosphere. Yet the most superb work eminates from so many classrooms, that educationalists, politicians, and parents are delighted and, in all honesty, astounded at the standards achieved. Of course purpose-built studios attached to every primary school would be welcomed by large numbers of teachers, but this is not a possibility and so young teachers must accept the general classroom environment in which they find themselves teaching.

In my many visits to schools in the United Kingdom and abroad, I have seen remarkably good lessons actually undertaken in narrow, over-crowded corridors and school entrance halls because of lack of teaching space, and have been amazed at the high standards which were achieved in those adverse and difficult conditions. Yet this has never worried me for I believe that the good teacher will be successful anywhere – even in a dilapidated barn or a wind-swept meadow – although I must agree that well-planned, purpose-designed classrooms with up-to-date facilities will help all teachers to achieve more success.

There are still numerous classrooms in old nineteenth century schools in use in Britain today which lack essential items such as sinks, decent cupboard space, display boards or adequate lighting. Some are in noisy, dirty downtown areas, others in small villages in remote country districts. In contrast, many modern, purpose-built classrooms contain everything required for teaching art, making practical work much easier to plan for. Some have separate 'workshop' areas adjacent to them inside the building as well as having useful areas outside where work can spread out to. Obviously, good working facilities are a tremendous help, but the main criterion on the part of the teacher is the 'right' attitude. An excellent teacher will provide a flourishing education anywhere, while a weak one will constantly make excuses for poor teaching and would have difficulty in a splendid palace.

What about the planning of suitable primary art work? What should be considered? What should be done? Graduates are now being trained to teach in nursery (pre-school), infant, and junior schools and, through their degree studies, are generally subject specialists. Previously, primary teachers undertook a more generalized course of training which tended to emphasize 'children' as much as 'subject studies'. However, since present-day graduates have been strongly orientated to their specialisms, I feel there is a danger that they might find it rather hard to refocus their thinking towards 'children and how they learn'. I am of the opinion that as highly intelligent people this will raise little, if any, difficulty. In teaching art they must ensure that children are provided with a variety of interesting materials. This will enable their pupils to explore as many art materials as possible empirically. But it is important that they inculcate in their pupils an ability to select 'suitable' materials for different tasks. This will not be easy to do after a number of years in specialist degree studies, especially as the realm of art will be somewhat strange to many of them.

The first thing a teacher must do is to look closely at the classroom itself, making a mental (or even a written) analysis of the situation. Is the room arranged well so that art and craft work can be engaged in easily by the children? Is there a sink in the room and is this adjacent to the working area for art studies? The teacher must not be put off if no sink exists. I recall in my second teaching post in an industrial town in Lancashire that I had no sink. Water had to be carried in buckets from the floor below and placed in large earthenware pots. It worked.

How much space will be devoted to art? Questions such as these – and others which will emerge – need thought. It is also important in teaching art at all the primary stages to ensure that children wear the appropriate dress. It is not practical for seven-year-old boys to do art in neat red blazers. These should be taken off and aprons or smocks (old shirts are a very good substitute) put on. Parents, quite rightly, may be angry if the children's clothes are messed up.

The point I am making is that teachers need to plan sensibly for every art activity in which their pupils engage. It is important to establish:

- the suitability of a particular art and/or craft and/or design activity for a child's age and stage of development (It is no use expecting a

19

Plate 4   This young artist is painting vigorously. He is well protected by his overall and this allows him to concentrate hard on what he is doing.

child of five to be able to cast a model of a donkey in bronze.)
- the type of clothing to be worn for a specific art activity at any time
- the number of children who are able to be involved in an activity – not too many and not too few
- whether a child is simply repeating the familiar (we all like to do this and there are times when it is important to permit it to happen) when, it fact, he or she should be engaging in different and/or new educational experiences or, indeed, whether 'repeat' experiences will strengthen knowledge skills and confidence
- what new skills you want a child to learn from a particular activity in relation to what the child has done before (most important at the junior level where the teacher can so easily bore children by repeating

unthinkingly what the children have done once or a number of times before in their infant schools)
- how an art activity or art activities fit into integrated projects, if at all
- when to teach aspects of art as a discreet subject

I indicate these fundamental criteria as a basis for sound thinking in the planning of art work. Teachers will need to add others arising from their daily experiences. What is absolutely crucial, however, is the need to maintain a flexible attitude. The teacher must have a respect for young children – bearing in mind at all times their levels of skill, their interests and wider curricular concerns which he or she knows to be important to the children's education. A balance must be retained between teacher interests and child interests; between one subject and another; between one skill and another; between experimentation and direct activities – and this is where experience in teaching, knowledge of children, as well as knowledge of subject areas across the curriculum are important.

The kinds of materials which may be used

Teachers are not always in a position to decide which art and craft materials they would like to have in their classrooms, although those with imagination and an entrepreneurial spirit will always find ways and means to acquire what they need. Some schools have an all-purpose buying policy, purchasing materials from art suppliers and keeping these in a central store under the headteacher's charge. Classroom teachers then have to make specific requests for materials as and when they require them. Most British Local Education Authorities now belong to local consortia – which are groupings of LEAs and suppliers, comprising committees consisting of LEA advisers, headteachers, teachers, art suppliers and LEA officers meeting at regular intervals throughout the academic year to discuss their requirements and to decide the quality of materials and equipment on offer. Individuals on these committees are able to make suggestions and to offer advice and help with respect to what is required in both primary and secondary schools throughout the region served by any one consortium. The use of consortia has led to the bulk buying of large quantities of materials and equipment, making it far cheaper for LEAs to buy and distribute to the schools under their control. If schools were to buy direct from large or small suppliers they would certainly find their purchases much more expensive. Primary

Inspectors/Advisers and Specialist Art/Craft, Design and Technology (CDT) Inspectors/Advisers are normally involved with Consortia Committees, bringing specialist knowledge and experience to discussions and decision-taking in the hope that the 'right' kind of provision results. Unfortunately, many of the materials obtained 'cheaply' in this way are sometimes of inferior quality, and I have known teachers complain about this. Perhaps a happy compromise is for a headteacher to insist that some 'better quality' materials be purchased directly by a school if, and when, these are required for specific work.

Young teachers must seek advice from their headteachers or senior and more experienced colleagues as to 'what' to request in the way of art materials and equipment. Their colleagues will be only too pleased to be of assistance, and will undoubtedly have used a wide range in their own teaching so that they can offer advice based upon experience. LEA Inspectors/Advisers, too, are there to offer guidance – particularly on their in-service courses and conferences – while most LEAs publish working papers and curriculum guidelines, lists of materials and other valuable information.

As a general rule the following materials will be useful in the teaching of all manner of work in art, craft and design (others may be added by individual teachers or schools depending upon the kind of work which is done):

Supports
paper (various types and colours)
- drawing paper (for drawing, painting, printing)
- cartridge paper (for drawing, painting)
- sugar paper (for general work because of cheapness)
- cover paper (for general use and display)
- crêpe paper (for pattern-making and decorative work)
- tissue paper (for pattern work and display)
- newspaper (for general use)
- brown and coloured wrapping papers (general)
- poster papers (for printing and display)

card (a range of types and colours)
- thin card for model making
- thicker card for model making & mounting
- kitchen waste (cartons) for model making

Painting materials
paints
- powder paints (for general purposes)
- ready-mixed colours (for painting, patterning, printing and model colouring)
- water colours (for producing washes)
- finger paints

brushes
- hog hair brushes (large and small)
- water colour brushes (large and small)
- plastic spatulas

palettes
- special painting palettes (usually illustrated in catalogues)
- tin and plastic lids
- plastic beakers
- old plates and saucers

Drawing materials
pencils
- hard (H) and soft (B) pencils
- coloured pencils
- charcoal pencils

crayons
- coloured wax crayons
- conté crayons
- oil pastels

charcoal
- sticks of charcoal
- charcoal pencils

chalks
pastels
felt-tipped pens
- black
- coloured

fibre tipped pens
ball-point pens

Printing materials
inks
- improvised inks made from various paints, drawing inks and dyes
- non-waterproof printing inks

rubber-covered rollers

inking-up slabs
- pieces of paper, card, hardboard, formica, glass, etc.

Adhesives
various classroom glues, pastes, gums and cements
- adhesives of various types

Model-making materials
constructional materials
- card
- paper
- wood
- string
- wire
- plaster
- canes (from garden centres)

carving materials
- soap
- wood
- plaster
- dried clay

modelling materials
- clay
- plasticine
- papier mâché

weaving materials
- various fibres and threads
- string
- wool
- raffia
- paper strips
- kitchen foils

This list is not extensive but should serve as a useful resource or at least a working basis for taking action. Catalogues of school art materials can be obtained from large suppliers of school materials, and these are full of the most interesting and valuable information. Sometimes headteachers will make special requests for items which are not on Consortium lists so that project work can be carried out, and will contact the suppliers direct. School funds – obtained through the efforts of teachers in running jumble sales and school fairs – often make such requests possible.

It is perfectly understandable that LEAs and schools are anxious to obtain materials in bulk and from the cheapest sources, for their budgets are limited. However, I feel that this is not entirely a good thing and could be a two-edged sword. Sometimes children deserve to experience 'the very best'. I would therefore advocate that occasionally a teacher must give a child top-quality materials with which to work, using the maxim that it is only possible 'to bake a good cake with good ingredients'. One or two good-quality artist sable brushes could be held by the teacher so that children could experience their use. I sometimes did this when I taught in schools and found children – even those with little interest – responding in an amazing way. Their respect for 'real' artists and 'proper' artist's equipment soared and they tended to have an increased pride in using good brushes. The same applied with other top-quality pieces of equipment or, for example, the occasional sheet of hand-made paper. The quality of the work also improved and with it their own evaluation of what they achieved. As an artist I always find it a pleasure to use the very best materials. When as a calligrapher and illuminator I use gold leaf, I get an enormous thrill. If I use gold ink there is no thrill, simply a kind of flatness of response. This proves to me that the best materials (and equipment) add an indefinable quality to my own artistic experiences and the work I do, and it stands to reason that young children will enjoy similar experiences if given the opportunities. Painting with the fine sable brush and egg-tempera colours made from fine levigated powder colours and glair is a joy which I would compare to the playing of a concert grand piano. Painting with a poor quality, cheap classroom nylon brush and powder paint must be like hammering a tuneless, honky-tonk bar-room upright. *Quality raises quality* and so it is occasionally worth any extra expense entailed. Give children the best and the best will be forthcoming!

What art experiences do children need to have?

It has already been established that children need extensive, and I would add intensive, experiences of doing art and thinking about art. They need to work in both two and three dimensions so that they experience and better understand flat imagery (2D) and spatial form (3D). On this point, HM Schools Inspectorate says:

> Art and craft are included in the curricula of all primary schools;
> HM Inspector's survey found that children would benefit if their

work were based more often than it is on direct observation and study. Their work should encourage the development of skills and inventiveness in producing artefacts. More emphasis than at present should be placed on work in three dimensions and some of this might be of a simple technological kind aimed at designing and making things that work. Art and craft are often usefully associated with other aspects of learning, for example topics in history and geography, but they are also valuable in their own right as a vehicle for individual expression.

(Department of Education and Science Welsh Office 1985: 12)

Plate 5 The time and care spent in displaying work well will encourage children while at the same time giving them a real sense of achievement. Lettering which is well done and legible makes displays much more worthwhile and will take little extra time and effort.

Teachers must, then, try to ensure that their pupils work in the following areas of experience:

Drawing – looking, recording and expressing.

Colouring – basic colour-mixing in the painting of pictures and patterns, as well as models and sculptured forms.

Modelling — creating 3D objects with plastic materials (e.g. clay, plasticine).

Constructing – with resistant materials such as wood, wire, metal, plastics, etc.

Texturing – with all manner of 2D and 3D materials.

Patterning – repeat patterns with drawing, printing and painting materials or even printing on textiles; rubbings.

Printing – patterns, pictures, maps, illustration, books, charts and textiles.

Weaving – with paper, threads, cloth, etc.

Computing – where equipment and software is available – creating computer imagery.

Problem-solving – in a whole range of art/craft/design activities involving the processes of: thinking (conceiving ideas); experimenting (to discover appropriate materials and solutions); rationalising (solutions in design terms); and evaluating and criticising (possibly through discussion and writing).

Looking, criticising and appreciating – by means of research (in art books, libraries, art galleries, museums, etc); meeting artists/craftspersons and designers; discussion; talks.

These areas of experience are, inevitably, interrelated for they depend upon knowledge and mastery of 'handling and making' skills and techniques, and upon 'aesthetic, appreciation and designing concepts' which embrace the children's own interests or the motivation which their work in art gives them. The Leicestershire Education Committee's Guidelines (1982) explains this quite succinctly:

> a teacher might want her pupils to become more aware of surface textures and patterns in the world around them and how texture can be used in art. This could be done in a very concrete way by examining the texture of particular objects – bark, leaves, stones, feathers, fur, etc. and later this could lead to the representation of texture through marks, e.g. brush strokes, marks with pencils, pastels, crayons, etc. This again might lead to textural work in clay

or collage. The ways in which 'real' artists have used texture could also be considered.

Texture is a visual and tactile quality. Other examples of visual qualities are shape, colour, tone (light/dark), space, line, contrasts. Visual and tactile qualities are everywhere in the world which surrounds us. They are also the qualities or elements which we must use, control and exploit when we express ourselves through the use of art materials.

So in devising a structure for art teaching in the primary school, we need to keep in mind a number of interrelated aspects. It may be helpful to attempt to summarise the most important of these:

1 *Child development:* Stages in the creative and mental growth of the child – our teaching must be related to the child's capabilities and needs. (The way in which children draw gives a helpful indication of their developmental level.)

2 *The motivation of the child:* What moves him/her to want to draw, paint, model, etc. There should be scope for the children's personal ideas as well as work stemming from group or class projects. First-hand sensory experience and sensitive observation are important.

3 *Media and materials:* Their possibilities and limitations. Successful expression (rather than disappointment and frustration) depends on confidence, understanding and skill in the handling of materials and media. It is sometimes helpful to restrict the available media – to explore a particular material or technique in depth. (On the other hand, it would be desirable to work towards a situation where the child was able to choose from different media and select what he felt at home with – or through which he could best express his idea.)

4 *Basic elements of art:* Visual and tactile qualities such as line, shape, colour, tone, texture, space and contrasts which present themselves to the senses and which are integral components in the use of art media. Growing understanding of these visual and tactile elements involves the formation of concepts: the development of 'visual literacy'.

5 *Art appreciation and critical skills:* Encouraging children to look thoughtfully and sensitively at works of art and design and to try to discover something about their quality, purpose or meaning. Critical and 'looking' skills are not only valuable in themselves but also as important tools which children need to use in their own art work.

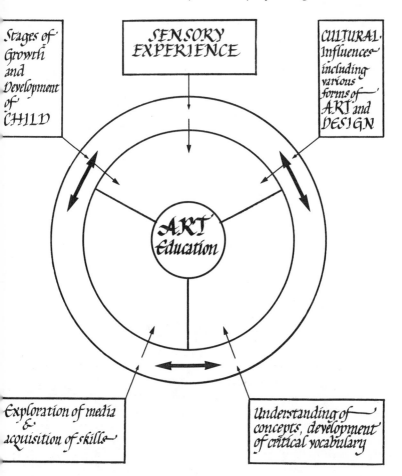

Figure 2   Interrelated aspects of art education. (See Leicestershire Education Committee's *Guidelines*, 1982.)

The inter-relationship of art aspects can be seen in Figure 2.

Problem-solving activities

The educational value of art, craft and design activities of a problem-solving nature cannot be stressed too much, for they are an important

29

aspect of the creative/aesthetic domain of learning. In employing this form of learning the teacher will ensure that children:

1 give consideration to the kinds of task they are asked to do or decide for themselves to engage in
2 be placed in a situation where they will have to think deeply and rationally about one or more problems
3 decide upon a strategy (or strategies) through which to solve the problem(s)
4 choose for themselves (albeit with teacher help) appropriate materials and designing-making methods which they hope will lead to a solution of the original problem(s) – while being aware that new or different ones may arise as they work
5 make, on conclusion, assessments of their achievements and their working strategies

In their previous, and other on-going, art work they will have become conversant with a range of materials which affect their sensory

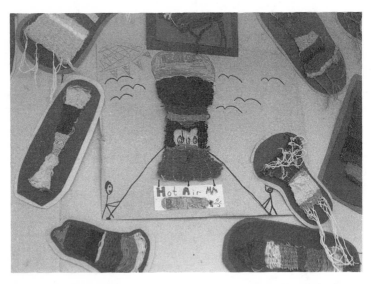

Plate 6   Simple exercises in weaving. This craft work introduced the class to the use of coloured threads and craft skills.

perceptions and experiences, the use of which will be developing their manual skills and inventiveness. These will then be applied confidently when they engage in problem-solving work.

The children's natural desire to manipulate materials in an inventive way shows, as noted earlier, their inborn 'originator instinct' (Buber 1961). These natural instincts give children an extremely strong, urgent desire to reorganize objects and images in different and often, for them, new ways. They will design with materials. They will sketch. They will build with plastic or wooden bricks or constructional materials, weaving imaginative thoughts into what they produce. Her Majesty's Inspectors of Schools, writing on this matter, say of children:

> Their work should encourage the development of skills and
> inventiveness in producing artefacts. More emphasis than at present

Plate 7   Children are able to make simple tiles with clay. Here we see examples which have been suspended from a classroom ceiling to form a kind of mobile.

31

should be placed on work in three dimensions and some of this
might be of a simple technological kind aimed at designing and
making things that work.
(DES 1981: 12)

The DES stress that much more work should go on concerned with
skills, inventiveness, three dimensions and CDT: this concept cannot be
repeated often enough.

It is encouraging that primary art and technology increasingly
embraces problem-solving activity work. Children could be given a
simple task to do which, for example, might be a suggestion that they
construct a bridge across the gap between two tables set 15in (30cm)
apart with tight rolls of newspaper, constructed in such a way that it is
strong enough to hold a heavy book upon it. In fact this is not an easy
task. It is one which will bring the children right into the realms of
technology. It will demand a need to think, to plan, to design, to make
and to assess the resulting structure and its effectiveness – i.e. will it
hold the book? In working on this idea the children will be in the
situation of being architects, engineers, and designers: a situation
demanding decision-making and aesthetic judgements. They might then
be in a better position from which to judge the design and construction
of a local railway bridge.

The whole area concerned with designing and making activities in
primary education is an increasingly important one. General classroom
teachers may lack the necessary knowledge and expertise, and who can
blame them if they view it as a specialist area demanding specialist
training and experience. But what can the schools do? They must rely
upon their teachers to fulfil this role and to employ appropriate
teaching strategies. If an LEA decides to cluster schools, so that teacher-
expertise is shared by teachers working in a number of schools, this
could be beneficial. The ideal might appeal to teachers who wish to
specialize rather more although, of course, a 'clustered' teaching force
would need to be balanced in what it offers to its group of schools.

Some schools will be in the fortunate position of being able to invite
local craftspersons to talk to their pupils about the way in which they
set about a designing and making task in their own craft. Even a brief
contact with a builder, a thatcher, a bricklayer, a blacksmith, an
architect or a landscape gardener working for the local public parks,
will have a profound impact upon the children and be extremely
beneficial in stimulating interest and knowledge of design-related
procedures which they might usefully adapt at classroom level.

In 1987 the Design Council produced a report defining design as 'the way in which we try to shape our environment, both in its whole and in its parts'. When children engage in artistic pursuits embracing designing and making they, too, are doing just this. And in doing so, boys and girls will 'be trying to mould materials, space, time, and other resources which are available to meet a need he or she has identified' (The Design Council 1987: section 3 para. 3.3). At times the teacher may be the one to make an identification, although it is better if the children do this themselves. This report notes three basic designing and making criteria:

1   a requirement to listen to suggestions made by others as to how a problem might be tackled
2   the need to consider other pupil's ideas about how any solution fulfils the envisaged function
3   that design-related problems require the exercise of discrimination

Plate 8   Children are now quite skilled at using computers and, as here, can employ existing programmes designed for a range of curriculum studies. They should also be encouraged to experiment by 'painting' and 'drawing', using the monitor screen as a substitute for artwork.

and do not simply lead to a predetermined 'right' solution which the teacher has decided upon (para. 3.4).

The Primary Working Party of the Design Council also stressed that design-related activities are not the prerogative of any age group but can be undertaken at any stage in primary schooling. These criteria are a helpful guide in the planning of simple classroom procedures concerned with design education, particularly with respect to those embracing co-operative learning and the tackling of design-related problems.

I have met teachers who were keen to involve their pupils in this kind of work but who said they couldn't think of what to do. There is no need to take this attitude, for ideas on design work are plentiful. Some ideas need only be very simple, others may be of a highly complex nature demanding a high level of constructive thinking and involvement.

If the teacher bears five developmental stages in mind when thinking about and operating problem-solving work, then things should go ahead smoothly. The problem-solving stages I propose are:

Stage 1   Planning

- posing the problem – ideas, reasons and possible theoretical outcomes
- consideration of ways to set about tackling the problem
- discussion (small groups and/or class-based)
- consideration of materials required
      practical 2D/3D materials and equipment
      resource materials
      possible visits to be planned to galleries, libraries, factories, churches, etc.
- choosing work tasks or allocation of these to individuals and/or small working groups

Stage 2   Involvement/engagement/activity

- work experience – initial experimentation
- writing, reading, researching, discussion
- practical work activity
- use of notebooks, sketch pads, films, videos, etc.
- discussion and assessment
- illumination of new ideas thrown up by the project work so far
- consideration of unforeseen problems and difficulties
- pointers for planned and/or new lines of development

Stage 3   Development

• further involvement, discussion, evaluation and development

Stage 4   Possible solution

• rationalization of work done
• presentation through some visual or other means

Stage 5   Evaluation

• assessment of the success or otherwise of the project (did it achieve what it set out to achieve?) – (all participants would be involved, including teachers and pupils
• assessment of individual contributions
• assessment of small group contributions
• discussion of possible future developments

It is always fascinating to give different groups of children the same task, for they will undoubtedly come-up with different solutions. This is an interesting thing to do within any one class, but even more interesting if it is possible to carry it out with different age-groups. All problem-solving activities lead to invaluable discussion in which pupils say why they did what they did and how successful they were at doing it. What is also important is that their involvement in practical designing will increase their awareness of the designing and making which is going on all around them in the world today, as well as helping them to make considered appraisals of the design of major features such as roads, railways, theatre, theatre sets, or shopping malls. It will increase their interest too, in the natural world of designing and making in which animals and birds construct dams in streams or nests in trees. An interesting and thought-provoking suggestion which might be put to a group of children doing nature studies concerned with birds might be: 'Go outside and find some nest-making materials. Now what I want you to do is to build a nest like this robin's nest, yourself. Make it in a small tree outside of the classroom window – and use only your mouth.' This suggestion might cause some consternation. It would certainly stimulate a lot of active thought and then much more admiration for what a bird achieves.

This area of curriculum involvement impinges to a large extent upon the kind of learning a child would get from CDT, which is concerned with the design and making of things which work. CDT demands the use of more complicated equipment, experienced knowledge and skills which are usually associated with secondary schooling. Many junior children, particularly those in the older classes, find it a fascinating area and it might be possible to give them opportunities to have basic experiences and problem-solving activities which could lead them through gently to the kind of studies which they are likely to encounter when they go on to their secondary schools.

It is relatively easy to make some basic CDT tools and equipment available at primary level including, say, a bench, a vice, a hammer, a saw, some nails, and so on with which simple craft work can be done. Craft Advisers will offer guidance, as will local secondary teachers responsible for CDT. Teachers might also approach the Crafts Council Education Services Section (Crafts Council, 12 Waterloo Place, Lower Regent Street, London SW1Y 4AU, Tel: 01 930 4811), whose role is to support the place of the crafts in educational provision and to enhance the experience of students and teachers through contact with practising craftspeople and their work. The Crafts Council offers a comprehensive service which includes: an exhibition service, an information centre, an index of craftspeople, a slide library and loan service, open evenings, lectures, seminars, touring exhibitions, education resource packs, and a collection of contemporary crafts, and has a Crafts Council shop situated in the Victoria and Albert Museum in London. One of its excellent schemes is to arrange for craftspeople and artists to work in schools, which is a stimulation and encouragement to pupils, giving them a first-hand insight into the way art and craft is made by professionals. The Council also offers a publication service – including *Crafts Magazine* – and although its services are perhaps more relevant to secondary schools, interested primary teachers might find the Council's information extremely useful.

It is possible to get primary pupils to consider and engage in purposeful design projects, and as an example I should like to outline one which a teacher in the north of England gave to his class. His pupils were rather unhappy about their gerbils' cage, which they said was uninteresting for these small animals, and they asked if they could make a bigger more exciting one in which the animals would have room to play. Having given this idea a few evenings' thought, the teacher agreed, seeing a project of this kind as an interesting and educationally important one if it could be planned and executed well. As a result he got every pupil in his junior class involved, splitting them into six groups and asking each group to tackle the designing and making (problem-solving) task in their own way.

The project: design a living environment for two gerbils

This gerbil house must be based upon studies of gerbils, their needs and habits. It should contain 'play' structures. The following stages must be followed:

1 Preliminary research (A)

Study the gerbils in their cage for periods of ten minutes, three times each day for five days and make notes and drawings based on your observations. These will be used in discussions as to how your design will proceed.

2 Discussion

Discuss, as a small team of designers, what you intend to do, what materials you will require and how to set about making the new environment.

3 Planning

Draw plans of the proposed living environment, to scale, as well as elevations and sketches. Base these on your research findings and discussions.

4 Discussions

Hold further planning meetings.

5 Production

Having selected and obtained relevant materials and tools for making the environment, go on to construct it, but consider its scale and where it will be kept in the school.

6 Completion and research (B)

When you have completed your model, introduce the two gerbils into it. Does it work? Do the gerbils seem happy living in it? Are they happier than they were in their cage? These – and other – questions which you must think about are important and mean that you will have to do a second piece of research by monitoring the behaviour of the gerbils for three ten-minute periods each day for one week.

7 *Evaluation*

Compare the research notes and observations obtained in the first research period (A) with those from the second research period (B) and seek answers to these relevant questions: Do these two gerbils appear to have a better place in which to live? Do they have *more* or *less* interesting things to do? Is the new environment that you have designed and made a success? If it is, why is it a success?

The teacher involved in the project was delighted with the outcome of this problem-solving exercise and considered it successful. It aroused interest in the living habits of gerbils (not art, but nature study). It stimulated many thoughtful ideas. It resulted from good co-operative learning and working sessions. It gave the group a set of sequential stages through which to proceed at their own pace and to bring the project to a succesful conclusion.

As a designing/making exercise it involved: (a) rational thinking, simple research to throw up facts which would help designing and making; (b) the wise selection and use of relevant materials and methods of working (involving practical skills and use of tools) in producing the gerbils' environment; and (c) self-assessment and evaluation of the exercise and the final product.

Stimulus from the world around us

The everyday world abounds with a tremendous richness and variety of visual imagery and if children learn to use 'discerning' eyes, they can sift through it carefully and selectively before using it to stimulate art work in all kinds of materials. The immediate surroundings cannot fail to inspire both individual and group activities of an artistic kind, and they also provide material for project work which embraces a number of curricular aspects so that learning experiences are 'real' while also being seen to be much more relevant than many arising from textbook prescriptions. Yes, the environment provides a ready-made, easily available feast, but we must see that our pupils do not gorge themselves so that they simply get mental and visual indigestion – we must encourage them to be selective so that they digest their visual experiences wisely.

Plate 9   Nature study projects often require an ability to draw and paint and this shows that art has a part to play in such work.

The world around is obviously a confusing mix of both natural and man-made forms, forms which come in diverse shapes, sizes, colours, patterns, structures and textures. These may often appear to be chaotic and in meaningless disarray, so selection and re-ordering – in an artistic/design sense – will be needed. But the environment is certainly very exciting, and it stimulates interest and thought and, as teachers, we must constantly remind ourselves of certain questions. These might include:

* what should children look at?
* what should they look for?
* how, in considering art studies, should we ourselves proceed?

I wonder, in thinking about the use of environmental stimulus, if the secret lies in simply knowing *how* to be selective and knowing *what* to use from the surrounding world: a world which I see as a chaotic visual symphony. Mature artists perfect their own techniques, of course, as they develop personal discernment or what Paul Klee (an early twentieth-century artist and art professor) considered to be 'thinking eyes', which are sometimes dismissed simply as artistic intuition by

39

those who are artistically uneducated. This is certainly a false premise, for the skill of working with thinking and seeing eyes can be learned and developed. Children can then learn how to use their eyes and can be taught how to see. They can be trained to be observant so that they are aware of the visually-exciting aspects contained in the environments in which they are immersed each day. They can develop an ability to sharpen their visual senses by focusing upon countryside landscapes or town panoramas or, in contrast, on relatively small areas within their own classrooms, and then be asked to use their eyes effectively.

A lot is to be learned simply by looking closely at pieces of natural form. The lines, shapes, patterns and textures in pieces of wood will be given a much greater impact if children make rubbings of them with black or coloured wax crayons on white paper. Alternatively, they could make rubbings with white crayon on white paper and brush ink across to produce a 'wax resist' effect. Then they might go on to ink-up an old piece of broken railing with a roller and black ink so that they can take a number of prints from it. If you look at the repeat print of the wooden railing it forms a kind of landscape. With a little imagination this could be given other features such as trees, pylons and houses – printing these with the edge of a small piece of card or painting them in with a small brush. Children tend to have far more imagination than an adult and would suggest many more original ideas.

A cursory glance is not good enough. Children must look carefully; they must then look again; and possibly again, for only in practising looking will they really learn how to see, to discover and to understand.

Plate 10   Looking closely at the lines, shapes and patterns in pieces of wood can teach a lot about natural form.

Perhaps this should be coupled with the development of the ability to retain vivid mental pictures of what they see, and to store these in their minds for future reference. This can be aided by the ability to record visually – by means of drawing, painting, photography or even cinephotography – so that individual development and curriculum work is enhanced. At first, however, it is often quite sufficient for children to have pleasurable visual experiences simply for their own sake. Such experiences might be seeing magnificient sunsets, lovely flowers, tyre tracks on a muddy road, patterns on a butterfly's wings or the arrangement of match sticks in a simple pattern, experiences which are of a completely aesthetic nature. Sometimes experiences such as these will lead the children on to a range of artistic work and they might paint pictures, produce prints and drawings, design books or make constructional models so that their 'thinking', 'seeing' eyes complement their 'making' skills to good educational effect.

In order to encourage children to use their eyes effectively the teacher could start by making arrangements of carefully displayed objects in the classroom. A few shells, seed heads, pebbles (of various size, colour, and texture), or dried flower heads arranged in a row on a sheet of white paper will immediately capture the children's attention. They will look at such things, pick them up to examine them closer and ask questions. A magnifying glass will increase their interest and the only difficulty will be to curb their bubbling excitement. In order to augment a small display like this one it might be a good idea to have some books, magazines, photographs and even slides close by to help the children to identify and classify the natural objects being scrutinized.

Some objects will lend themselves better to vertical rather than to horizontal display. Others will be far too large for classroom use and in this case the teacher will have to rely upon visual means to show them to the children. These might include man-made structures – castles, skyscrapers, ships, electricity plyons, and so on. On the other hand, minute forms which the naked eye would have difficulty in identifying could be brought to the children's notice by means of a microscope. Whatever the objects, whether large or small, whether living or of an inanimate nature, children will be fascinated and their educational development will be enriched and widened.

3

Planning what to teach

The balance between 2D and 3D work

A great deal of school art has, traditionally, been restricted to two dimensions. The reasons for this may be several: lack of knowledge, experience, and confidence on the part of teachers; the relative cheapness of 2D materials compared with bought 3D materials; the easier management of 2D materials and work; and the bulkiness of some 3D objects which makes their storage a problem. As a result, two-dimensional work has tended to predominate.

It is important to set this situation right. Teachers must attempt to provide a balance between the two by trying to ensure that pupils have opportunities to experience a range of both 2D and 3D work. They might find it helpful to design a simple 'record card', which could then be photocopied, based on the idea shown in Figure 3.

Work in the three-dimensional aspect need not be costly, for household waste – card (food cartons), tins, newspaper, wrapping paper and plastic – costs nothing, and is ideal for a lot of work (see Lancaster 1988a). Scrap materials have long been used in schools. All that is required is an inventive thought or two, and incredibly interesting work will result. In doing *two-dimensional work* children in primary schools will:

- experience and gain an understanding of a range of materials used in its production
- learn relevant manual skills and techniques in using materials and basic equipment competently
- experience how to use the basic elements of a visual grammar
- become increasingly proficient as young designers
- learn how to draw and paint (from observation) all manner of environmental phenomena
- experience the joy of self-expression through 2D forms of visual communication

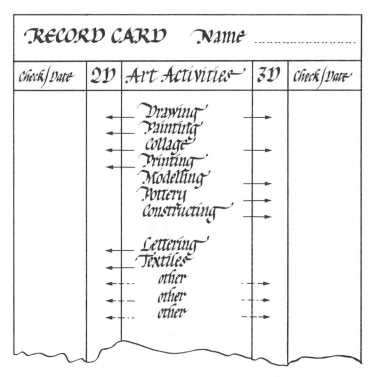

RECORD CARD   Name ....

Check/Date	2D	Art Activities	3D	Check/Date
←		Drawing	→	
←		Painting	→	
←		Collage	→	
←		Printing	→	
		Modelling	→	
		Pottery	→	
		Constructing	→	
←		Lettering		
←		Textiles		
←		other	→	
←		other	→	
←		other	→	

Figure 3   A record card.

Work can be stimulated by both teacher and pupil interests; by collections of natural and man-made things; by photographs, slides and pictures by artists; by visits; by holidays; and by many other means, while educational work in other subjects will often promote further ideas.

In doing three-dimensional work primary children will:

- develop a meaningful understanding of 3D form and function
- understand better the characteristics of 3D materials such as wood, card, paper, yarn, thread, plastic, clay, stone, wire, cane, plaster, etc., which teachers get them to use in modelling, building, constructing, shaping and carving
- learn relevant manipulative skills and techniques, and gain confidence in using 3D materials and tools safely and competently

43

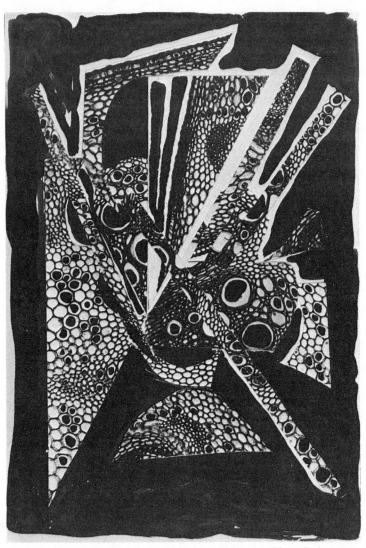

Plate 11   This exciting pattern was done by an eight-year-old pupil who cut up
a photocopy of a photomicrograph (a greatly magnified section through a
clematis stem by Douglas Lawson) and then arranged the pieces to form a
pleasing design. Black ink was added with a brush to give the design an added
interest.

44

- learn how to think in 3D terms
- engage purposefully in 3D designing and making problems which are essentially pragmatic and functional
- learn to appreciate with an increasing and informed understanding the artistic achievements of 3D artists such as sculptors, architects and potters in primitive, past and modern societies

Plate 12   The children who painted these landscapes had (a) gone out to make sketches on the spot, (b) used thick powder colours to obtain a 'painterly' effect.

The construction of models requires a high degree of skill and good eye, brain and hand co-ordination. Work of this kind is obviously valuable and through it the young person will learn about the inter-relationships of three-dimensional forms and structures. In later adult years he may find these experiences helpful when he designs, makes and fits a set of bookshelves in his house, or when he makes a rabbit cage or Wendy House for his own children. The educative value of designing and making project work is not always immediately apparent but can become meaningful in the most unexpected ways.

Constructional apparatus is used extensively in the infant sector. Children often use it imaginatively, working alone or in small groups, and this gives them opportunities to co-operate in designing and building experiences. What results is not of a permanent nature, of course, but is extremely valuable and informative with respect to spatial relationships and three-dimensional constructing.

Plate 13   The construction of models requires a high degree of skill and good eye, brain and hand co-ordination. These children are learning about the interrelationships of three-dimensional forms and structures.

Plate 14   Infants working with constructional apparatus, gaining valuable experience of co-operation in design and building.

Working with plaster of Paris calls for some expertise on the part of the teacher. An old shed or unused classroom, with water to hand even if this is only placed in buckets so that the material can be controlled, would be ideal for children tend to find that using plaster can be rather a 'messy' business.

Invigorating 3D work is invariably stimulated by classrooms containing collections and displays of both natural and man-made phenomena; photographs and slides of great cathedrals, churches, skyscrapers, oil rigs, bridges, space rockets, aircraft, small shells, grasses, spiders' webs, fruit, ferns, rocks and feathers; by a range of 3D tools, equipment and materials; and possibly by ideas cards which have been produced for classroom use.

47

Planning for schemes and lessons

The careful planning of teaching–learning schemes, projects, curricular activities, and single lessons cannot be stressed too much for it is crucial to their success. In order to achieve success the teacher needs to be thoroughly organized, and in planning for art will need to consider six important areas:

1   The project, theme or activity must be outlined clearly:

   ● what is it about?
   ● how long will it last? (half an hour; one day; one week; one term?)
   ● whether classroom-based only
   ● whether children will move into other parts of the school
   ● whether visits away from school will be required
   ● will other teachers participate?
   ● whether it follows on from other projects or work

2   The materials to be used by children will need to be obtained in advance to ensure a prompt start and progress. New or different materials and how they can be used will mean the children may need to be taught relevant skills and techniques.

3   The art and design elements to be embraced in the learning experience(s) encompassed by the art sessions must be identified. Will the children be concerned with *one* or more of these? (Colour, form, texture, pattern, shape, space, movement, form, etc) and what specific *aspects* (drawing, painting, printing, textiles, art history, sculpture, etc.) will they need to embrace or focus upon in carrying their work through?

4   Art and design functions, too, will have to be thought about and stated.

5   The purpose of the exercise and its aims and intentions must be considered.

6   As some projects and schemes will be of an integrated nature, the curricular connections have to be outlined so that the children understand these.

Planning sheets are invaluable aids, and an outline idea for one is given here. It is obviously more satisfactory if teachers design their own – perhaps using this one purely as a guide – and have a number available to make their organizing easier. This example has a section where

Plate 15   Plaster of Paris models under way in a room which has been set aside for this special craft form.

evaluation notes can be written and where essential comments and ideas for modifications or future plans may be added.

Drawing – a key element in art

Drawing is an important element of all aspects of art, craft and design for it is the vehicle through which 'thinking and designing' processes are germinated and, quite often, through which they are crystallized before being manifested in relevant materials and forms. It provides an

49

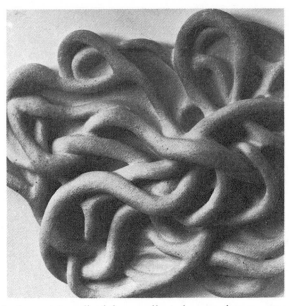

Plate 16 Intertwining rolls of clay can effectively create abstract patterns based upon the roots of shrubs. If a school possesses a kiln then models can be fired or even glazed.

invaluable discipline and skill for young children. In the nineteenth century, elementary school pupils made carefully observed copies of geometric figures, plants and flowers in drawing lessons which were repetitive and boring, but today there is much more freedom for individual expression, and drawing is a pleasurable activity through which children are able to externalize their ideas and thoughts.

Pre-school and infant children (nursery children and 5- to 7-year-olds) learn much by experimenting, and their 'play' is really 'work' experience in adult terms. They will explore different drawing materials (crayons, pencils, chalks, inks, and paints), and how 'mark-making' implements produce graphic images on paper. They have a wide range of materials to work with, and as a result they develop dexterity, confidence and graphic skill. This, of course, is also of tremendous help in developing their writing skills.

Junior pupils (7- to 11-year-olds) will obviously use the same materials and drawing implements as younger children, building upon

Project/theme/activity	Materials/skills/techniques
Art and design elements	Art and design functions
Aims (purpose)	Curricular connections
Evaluation and ideas for possible development	

Figure 4   A teacher's planning sheet.

their earlier experiences and developing their skills and ideas further. In these more advanced years they should be learning to look at things much more carefully, with 'thinking eyes', recording what they observe through the medium of drawing. They will also draw maps, models, plans, and mathematical figures. Observational drawing develops objective appraisal and understanding of the objects which are studied.

More mathematical drawing develops accuracy; while a combination of these will increase drawing skill and confidence. As children tackle problems of a designing nature they will carry through their preliminary drawing processes, bringing increasing experience and knowledge to their work.

Some ideas for expressive drawing

Children should, at every stage in their development, be encouraged to draw anything or to base their drawing on themes/ideas such as:

- people: mummy, daddy, the postman, astronauts, men from mars, sports people, etc.
- animals: my pet, a pussy cat, a cow, a tiger, a rabbit, etc.
- birds, fish, frogs, newts, etc.
- imaginatively conceived animals, birds and fish
- buildings: my house, a church, a castle, the garden shed, a shop, an oil rig, etc.
- trees: a big tree, a group of three trees, looking up into a tree, an imaginative view looking down from up a tall tree
- patterns: zig-zag patterns, compass patterns, pencil and ruler patterns, patterns in shells, etc

These are simply a few suggestions. Children themselves will suggest many more, while a few minutes' thought will bring an increasing number to mind.

Some ideas for observational drawing

The child's world abounds with a vast amount of material which they can draw. They should be encouraged to make collections for their classrooms so that a wide range of objects can be used in class sessions. Some children will take a great deal of pleasure in building up their own collections for 'home museums'. These will contain items such as:

- shells, rocks, stones and other natural objects which may be studied closely and drawn with pencils or pens
- these and other objects which can be examined under magnifying glasses so that they are considerably enlarged and then drawn
- a fern (or other leaf) which lends itself well to careful, mathematical

Plate 17 This boy is trying to obtain a likeness of himself by copying the image of his face in a mirror. In fact he is doing it rather well and is also managing to obtain a good interpretation of his striped jumper. Self-portraits are always useful in demanding that children try their best to explain in graphic terms, i.e. by means of drawing, exactly what they see.

measurement with rulers, protractors and compasses so that extremely accurate drawings are produced
- engine parts, old shoes, bicycles, old kettles, jumpers, lamps or other man made objects which are superb for close study

Some ideas for experimental drawing

It is important for children continually to experiment with the basic elements of drawing – with lines, dots and shading. They should also use as many different drawing implements as possible in order to discover for themselves what these will do. Telling children how drawing implements will perform is no substitute for their own experience, through trial and error, for real learning grows from experience. So, too, does real understanding. They might consider:

- heavy lines made to cover a sheet of paper
- drawing very thin, faint lines
- using dots to convey the impression of lines
- drawing closely-related wavy lines from the top to the bottom of the page
- doing more wavy lines – some thin, others thick and heavy
- pattern-making combining some or all of these ideas
- a pattern made from dots
- using 'slow' lines meandering over the sheet
- using 'vigorous' lines to convey speed
- drawing very big, strong shapes
- drawing small shapes
- drawing shaded shapes which are roundish or squarish

A few minutes' thought will produce many more ideas. Realize that experimental drawing is simply inventive mark-making on paper. It helps children to develop creative minds, manual dexterity and control. Consider drawings done in black and white, or white on black, coloured felt-tipped pens, or with brush and paints. Below is an idea for a story 'line' drawing that may be treated as a piece of fun and yet has serious educational undertones.

A story 'line' drawing

We all love stories, whether we are children or adults, and I have used them with young pupils, adolescents and adults to try to encourage creative art work of all kinds. It is fun to tell a story, but much more exciting to draw it as the story is told. In order to do this a class will require drawing paper and materials before the story begins. Having been provided with these, they could be told to draw as the story is told, for what they are going to do is to 'take line, dots and shapes for a walk', an easy enough thing for anyone to do. The instructions are as follows:

1 draw all the time the story is being told
2 draw with one or more of the drawing implements and/or materials provided

3   don't stop until the story ends

The story is simply made up. Here is a series of ideas:

A boy with spiky hair
Gets up out of bed
Goes downstairs and eats some breakfast
Looks out through the window and sees that it is raining outside
Goes out for a walk with a large umbrella
Walks down the country lane with trees on both sides
Comes to a big gate into a field
Climbs the gate and plods across the muddy field with heavy steps
Comes to a wood where tall, dark trees surround him
Sees a big wolf and is afraid
Turns and begins to run in a frightened way
Runs out of the wood, back across the heavy, muddy field
Is too tired to climb the gate
Manages to open it slowly
Plods down the lane
Goes into his garden, then in through the kitchen door
Flops exhausted into a chair near the fire

The resulting drawings will differ greatly. Some will be completely abstract in nature (patterns on the paper), while others will be representational. They could lead on to coloured drawings in felt-tipped pen.

Some ideas for observational drawing

A child can be given an object and asked to study it before attempting to render it as accurately as possible by means of drawing. This is an intensive exercise demanding concentrated effort and dexterity with graphic representation. The man-made object itself might be instrumental in determining the kind of drawing implement and materials to be used. In drawing a large wellington boot, for example, a child might draw boldly with a piece of screwed-up newspaper dipped into black ink; but in drawing a spider's web will have to use a fine pencil or mapping pen in order to produce the delicacy of line required to interpret the web's tracery.

Having previously experienced a range of drawing materials in an inventive way, the child should be able to make a sensible and knowledgeable choice. He or she will be selective so that the graphic rendering of the object will be as truthful to reality as possible. Some objects which children might draw are:

- cog wheels from clocks and watches – rendered freehand with pen and ink or drawn precisely with pencil and ruler
- leaves and plants – drawn vigorously with brush and ink or delicately with a pencil (sometimes with water-colour washes added)
- flower heads – drawn in ink on dampened paper, and with colour washes added for effect
- rocks and shells or feathers viewed through large magnifying glasses and drawn with ink and crayon, or painted with a fine brush
- a clematis branch – analysed, measured accurately and then drawn with the use of mechanical aids such as rulers, compasses and set-squares

Ideas are innumerable. Sometimes a rubbing of a piece of natural form will help a young pupil to understand the form itself better. The taking of a rubbing can precede the making of a careful sketch, or it can be done afterwards. A rubbing could be classified either as a 'drawing' or a 'print' (see Plate 18). At times the teacher will suggest ideas but at others a class will come up with many which can be used in art work. It would be an interesting exercise to ask a class to think of as many ideas as possible in five minutes. These could be written down, sorted out and

Plate 18   A rubbing of the skeleton of a fish, done with a soft wax crayon on A4 typing paper by a junior school girl. It was a rather difficult task, for the bones in the spinal column were raised much more than other bones, but it introduced the young girl to a different graphic skill while, at the same time, heightening her awareness and knowledge of natural patterns and arrangements.

then added neatly to an 'Ideas Book' which could be kept on a shelf in the art area.

Photomicrography might be a useful aid by means of which children could study and use the patterns of growth structures, the cellular forms of rocks, shells and plants, or the enlarged surfaces of the skins of fish. They might also use microscopes to enlarge the minutiae of nature so that they are then able to see more than simply using their naked eyes. On the other hand, a slide projector will throw greatly enlarged images on to large sheets of paper pinned to a classroom wall so that the children are then able to draw around them and to develop their large graphic images as paintings or patterns, on a scale normally denied them.

Nature is full of inspiration and has a plentiful supply of resource material just waiting to be used. When young artists look at natural forms they sharpen their visual and mental facilities, although a wise teacher will limit the discovery area for them, helping them to focus on interesting aspects so that they do not become confused or overwhelmed. A beach, for instance, is a vast expanse containing rocks, sand, pebbles, seaweeds, water, rock pools and countless other phenomena whose shapes, colours and surface textures can inspire an incredible range of art work back in school. But an individual child will find it much too bewildering – and should never be asked simply 'to draw a beach', which is a terrifying prospect even for a mature artist, and should limit his or her area of looking so that it can be more fully explored and used. To ask children to go out and make a sketch of a landscape is much too vast a problem for them to tackle. A teacher who does this is really being unfair to the pupils and it is far better to limit the subject by suggesting a smaller topic of interest. One way to do this is to give the children a cardboard mount. This can be attached to a garden cane with tape and placed in the ground. The pupil is then able to sit in front of the mount, which will define an area he or she has chosen, and draw exactly what is to be seen in it. One important factor to bear in mind in employing this method is that it seems to give children a lot more confidence as the mounts eliminate a vast amount of the environmental scene which is much too confusing, while narrowing the subject matter. Sketches may be transcribed into paintings, prints or collages.

The individual characteristics of an area of landscape will affect what children do. A rocky, barren-looking hillside might stimulate imaginative work of a dramatic type while a gently-flowing, rippling stream in a woodland glade will evoke a completely different effect.

Even a patch of waste ground in the heart of a dirty, noise-throbbing city will throw up its own stimulus and contain within itself many visual surprises and items which seem to be waiting to be depicted in pencil, chalk, ink or crayon.

Plate 19   The use of a cardboard mount as an aid in sketching the landscape helps the children to define an area and draw exactly what is seen in it. This girl was looking towards a group of trees and houses. The boy behind her was making a drawing that included part of a wire fence, the tops of the rose bushes, some tree branches and the roof of a house. Other children in the class found different pictures.

Some ideas for patterns

Observational drawing can go on into simple pattern-making, which might be done freehand or mechanically, to help children to develop graphic dexterity and confidence in their ability. It may be helpful, as an idea, to get them at times to focus upon *one* element. As an example, this could be line.

1   They could draw a range of lines of all kinds – thick, thin, wavy, bold, short and long – in an experimental and inventive way to increase their knowledge of linear qualities
2   They might then look at an object and, using lines only, make a representational image of it on paper – using similar lines to those discovered
3   Following this, they could take some of the linear elements from their object, or the drawing which has resulted, and create a drawn pencil, crayon or felt-tipped pen pattern

Plate 20   Photograph of a frosty cabbage. This kind of object will stimulate all manner of art work as it is unusual. It could encourage children to draw, to paint, to print, or even to make models in wire or papier mâché.

Other drawn patterns might be quite abstract in form. They could be based on straight lines, wavy lines or curved lines. These could be made to fit into certain shapes (e.g. a series of circles, squares or triangles), and some of these could be combined inventively. In some patterns it will be necessary to use rulers, compasses or other instruments, linking mechanical pattern-making with mathematical studies in a meaningful way.

Historical and cultural inspirations

Two invaluable sources of stimulus for curriculum studies work, including art, are historical and cultural aspects. These can help to link practical work while developing aesthetic awareness and art knowledge.

An example of how the study of a local village was used to inspire the entire curriculum of a small village school was illustrated by the BBC some years ago. A television programme was produced under the title 'Elizabethan Village', showing the children in a small village school in Worcestershire involved in an inspired learning situation. This entailed study visits to different parts of the village to examine carefully, for instance, a half-timbered cottage. The children drew it carefully (architectural studies), measured it (mathematics), considered what food would have been prepared and eaten in it in Elizabethan times (social studies and, as they prepared similar food later, cooking – home economics). They discussed how the Elizabethan people who lived there dressed, and made some costumes to wear in a play (historical dress-design); they discussed what music they had, which they listened to on record players as well as imitating themselves on instruments (music), and how servants were treated and where they slept – at the top of houses in draughty rooms, with a little straw for bedding (work studies). Other historical aspects of that age were introduced into their project work – ships, soldiers, sailors, monetary systems, religious beliefs and the social order of the village hierarchy. To assist them with their planning the teachers produced a flow-chart (Figure 5).

This was a broad-based, complete learning experience which the children were immersed in for a whole term. It relied upon a great amount of extra source material and culminated in displays, dramatic and musical functions, books and the BBC film. Art was a central and motivating force without which the project would have suffered and been weak. 'Elizabethan Village' was both a historical and a social study. It embraced the 'Great House' belonging to the local aristocracy

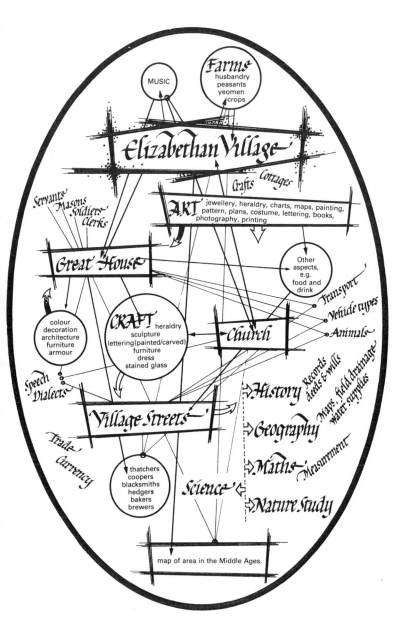

Figure 5   Flow chart of a topic based on an Elizabethan village.

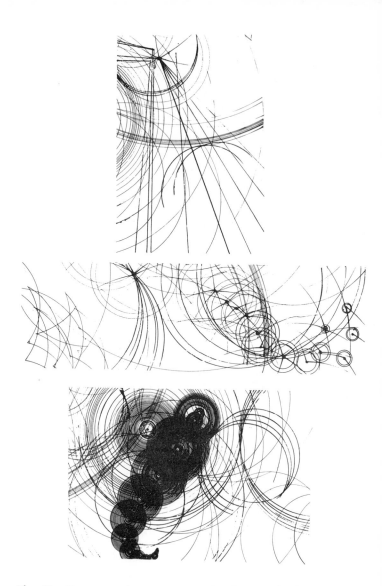

Plate 21 Compass-made patterns can produce linear work which is simple or complicated. Some children in a junior class were given compasses and asked to make 'experimental' patterns. Some added straight lines drawn with pens and rulers and the top example shows this clearly. Is this pure art? Is it mathematics? Are the children having worthwhile learning experiences? They certainly discovered a lot about curved lines, circles and the effects of criss-crossing or overdrawn lines and these, in my view, were educative things to learn about.

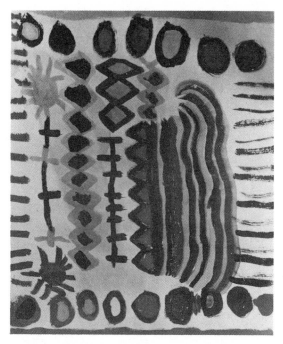

Plate 22   This painted pattern was done by a six-year-old pupil. It consists of
very direct and colourful brush strokes. These bold marks have, of course, been
carefully orchestrated by the child and show her concern for the picture space.
Indeed, the whole of the sheet of paper has been used well, with the linear
elements juxtaposed to give us a delightful 'visual tune'. The pupil could now
take the pattern idea further by developing a collage pattern with coloured
threads or, alternatively, by producing a pattern of rolls of clay on a clay tile.

of that age, and covered how they had acquired wealth and position.
The church and its history was studied, with the local vicar meeting the
children, showing them around and discussing its historical development
with them (this included architecture, carving, lettering, heraldry,
stained glass, church music and religion). Medieval strip farming was
discovered. Old tracks, lanes and roads were mapped. Hedgerows turned
up interesting plants, insects and animals, and local farmers offered
explanations for crop-growing and the kinds of tools which Elizabethan
farm-workers used.

   This is the kind of involvement/discovery theme which children can
experience anywhere. It can be in the middle of a town or at a port, in

Plate 23   A model made after a visit to see old sailing ships in an industrial museum, showing the children's fascination with masts and rigging.

Plate 24(a)   This dockland scene vibrates with interest. It could inspire a lot of creative work in art, including drawing with pencils, crayons, pen and wash or fine fibre-tipped pens; painting with inks and water-colour washes, of ships and reflections; lino and/or card line prints juxtaposed with washed areas of colour and texture; or even three-dimensional standing structures (small sculptures) in balsa wood and wire.

Plate 24(b)   Street scenes usually abound with street signs, lamps and cars which might inspire children to artwork involving designs and lettering, as well as the more usual pictures, drawings and prints. The construction of buildings varies greatly, some are built of timber and infilling (black and white), others have columns and porticoes, while others are more modern, inspiring children to model-making, perhaps.

contrast to a beautiful Worcestershire village, for similar learning potential will be there whatever the social environment.

Plate 23 shows a model made from rolls of newspaper and string by three children in a junior school. They had made a study visit to look at old sailing ships in an industrial museum in one of our largest ports and had become fascinated by masts and rigging. They decided not to make a model of a sailing vessel but to translate their sketch notes more liberally in constructing a standing linear structure. This work involved them with simple mathematical as well as art problems, and they found the construction of the model rather a difficult one. When the standing structure was completed, the pupils painted some of the rolled parts to make it more effective. An experience of this kind could teach children to appreciate masts and rigging on ships. They will begin to understand the difficulties encountered by ship builders and designers, whose task is to do with fitness for purpose, and they will have been involved in a useful and educative problem-solving experience embracing aspects of art, mathematics and CDT.

Present-day cultural differences might provide excellent material for educational studies. Since the last war minority ethnic groups have entered the country from many parts of the world, bringing with them a whole range of different religions, costumes, music, eating habits and languages. Inner city schools can tap this source easily, getting local minority ethnic craftsmen in to show art work from their countries of origin – these might include items like carvings, prints and dress fabrics. The same will be true for other groups, some of whom might be willing to dress up so that children can do paintings of them in brightly coloured costumes – an exciting experience for anyone.

4

Organizing art within the primary curriculum

Separate art: the value of pure art experience

As teachers, we can easily become over-obsessed with aims and purposes so that everything children do in school must in an educational sense, lead somewhere. I sometimes think it is a good thing to throw off this straight-jacket and to allow children the joy of pursuing a seemingly 'purposeless' activity for a short while. Why must there always be a reason for drawing lines and shapes, making a pattern, or producing a model? Surely a pure experience in art – or in dance or music – is enough in itself and should be encouraged? What do you do if a small boy wishes to paint blue spots all over a sheet of paper – stop him from doing so or encourage the child? If you attempt to stop the child, he might retort by saying that the day before you, the teacher, asked him to paint red lines within a circle. Answer that – or think about it.

I believe there are occasions when children will do things in art which have no apparent purpose to them. He or she will do so simply to satisfy an urge – which might be an inventive or creative urge but which, on the other hand, might have nothing to do with creativeness – and that in itself is purpose enough. This could be an emotional outlet or even an irrational action. It is aimless. But don't we all occasionally hum a tune as we dust, drive a car or walk in a country lane? Why? Simply because we want to do so. Ask yourself why a blackbird sings. He may have a purpose but often it seems that he does so for the sheer joy of doing it.

Do we need an explanation? Let children occasionally respond emotionally and sensitively to pure art experiences. Such response will be therapeutic and good for the soul. In this respect it has both an emotional and an aesthetic value and this can only be good for the child's well-being.

Linking art: topic and interest work across subjects

Much of this topic has been discussed elsewhere in this text and needn't be repeated. Art is a subject which has an in-built facility for linking well with other areas of curriculum work. It facilitates activity because of its focus upon 'making' and 'doing', and its immediacy is felt through visual and plastic imagery and form. The children's ability to manipulate materials in creating art work is brought into play in all manner of project work – whether this is pursued in other individual subject areas or in joint themes – when such skills are invaluable in bringing work to conclusion in a presentable visual form. Art is useful:

- in selecting materials, through experience, which will do what is needed
- in the arrangements of shapes on visual aids – designing
- in making objects of use in projects

Figure 6   'Art' as the central force in a project.

- in presenting materials well (including individual pieces of work, good titling, arrangement of texts, and presentation in exhibition or display form)

If children are accustomed to presenting work well through their art experiences, this will be seen in their cross-curricular projects. These will undoubtedly benefit from their aesthetic expertise and be more worthwhile. At times art will be the central motivating force in project work (see Figure 4), but on occasions it will act as a servicing agent only, and its function will simply be to enhance project work and materials visually.

If its role is a central one, art will motivate work by acting as an initiator of ideas. Examples of topics might be 'The Cathedral' (architecture, colour, pattern, texture, structure, etc) or 'Colour in dress' (studies of costume in Roman Britain, Regency England or the mid-twentieth century), to mention but two possibilities. Topics may be historical and art/design based, or they might look towards sub-cultural elements in our present-day society, for example 'Pattern in Indian artefacts', where everyday objects such as clothes, furniture, cooking utensils, jewellery, etc., are examined and brought into project work in display form, and then introduced into books made by children as a stimulus for their paintings, models, drawings, discussion and plays.

Four ideas for integrated project or theme work

A learning milieu which encourages cross-curricular learning is invariably a dynamic one in which the different aspects of curriculum work are seen to be vital components in the educational machine. Each aspect (or subject area) will set the lead at different times with the others in supporting roles, although in these four ideas I have, for obvious reasons, leaned towards art and given it a dominant place. If, however, I were to use these ideas in more than one teaching situation my approach would vary and I would give other aspects preference, depending upon the children's interests, the work which they had done previously, or simply, and for me the most important factor, concern for the individual child and not for specialisms.

In using project work or themes we can attempt to make provision for the sequential development of educationally meaningful ideas and, as far as art is concerned, must consider:

- whether the art activities generated by a particular integrated learning

Plate 25   This quayside scene is incredibly rich in visual imagery. It vibrates with interest: three-dimensional structures and forms, some of which are repeated as regular patterns, two-dimensional patterns, and the like. Where is this masted vessel bound for? What is its history? What cargoes has it carried over the years? Did it have something to do with Long John Silver and Treasure Island? Ideas for creative art are not hard to find here.

theme will result in sensitive, sincere, and worthwhile personal involvement
- whether sincere co-operative effort will be necessary if it is to be conducted seriously
- whether learning experiences will be shared effectively
- whether a project will be capable of worthwhile completion

So we must propose some basic goals and then select appropriate objectives geared to these goals; then we must ensure that both goals and objectives are available, considering effective and workable methodologies.

The four ideas I put forward here are: water; machines and mechanical movements; snow; and trees.

Water

This idea entails much personal discovery. The teacher would have to prepare carefully as well as providing a wide range of materials.

- Art

Drawing with various implements and materials
Experimentation with dampened paper and inks
Looking at water, images and reflections
Pattern-making with paints, crayons, collage, etc.
Photography and film-making – water in streams, puddles, running down a window pane, etc.
Expressive work (painting/print-making/collage, etc.) based on ideas of 'the sea', 'inland waterways', 'canals', 'docks', 'fishing ports', and even 'fish tanks in the classroom'
Reference to: places throughout the world where water is important
Looking at art works in which water is used

- Music

Discovering the kinds of sounds which water will produce:
  - running water
  - splashing water
  - dripping water
  - sinks emptying
  - waterfalls
  - rain (recorded on tape)

Making simple musical instruments using water – in containers (shaking/blowing/hitting), etc.

WATER.
an emphasis on
PERSONAL DISCOVERY

MUSIC

- Containers with water, sand, beans, etc., to produce sounds (experimental)
- Listening to dripping and running water
- Handel's 'Water Music'
- Vaughan Williams' 'Sea Symphony'

MATHEMATICS.

- Measuring (liquid containers)
- Volume (also displacement)
- Size (playground puddles, sinks, ponds, lakes, seas, rivers, etc.)
- Depth (puddles, sinks, canals, rivers, etc.)
- Displacement (bowls, sinks, boats, ships, etc.)

SCIENCE.

- Mineral content
- Animal, insect, fish and plant life
- Aquaria in classroom
- Rushes and other vegetation in ponds, streams, rivers, lakes, sea-shore and differences—also uses (baskets, paper, etc.)
- Water creatures
- Respiration, size, movement, etc.

ART "Reflections"

- Drawing with inks and crayons (observational studies/patterns)
- Painting – 'watery effects', 'patterns'
- Collage – 'patterns'
- Oil colours on water to produce prints
- Thick and thin colour
- Looking at and using scenes – canals, lakes, sea (visits/photographs)
- Masts, rigging – linear elements
- Plants and trees – linear elements and colour

GEOGRAPHY

- Effects of water on land and different areas
- Sand and water trays to explore empirically the action and effects of erosion
- Monsoons/tides/tidal waves/river flows/deserts, etc.
- Tracing of routes of rivers—sources to mouths and stages of development
- Movements of shipping

HISTORY

- Use of water through the ages
- Study of civilizations near to or even on water
- Use of mills, villages, ports
- History of canals—transportation, goods and lives of people concerned
- Use of canals today (revival/adaptation)
- Ships—masted, steam, etc.

MOVEMENT and DANCE

- Moving freely and imaginatively to sounds of liquids
- Moving and dancing to music evoking water
- Watching and interpreting flow of water (taps, hoses, streams, rain, fountains and waterfalls)
- Ripples

Figure 7 'Water' — an integrated project topic.

Making music in groups
Listening to music by Handel (*Water Music*), Vaughan Williams (*Sea Symphony*)

● History
The use of water by human beings throughout history
Studying the developments of civilizations near to water sources
The effects of water upon various societies
Village life and water mills
Irrigation in agriculture
History of water transport – canals, rivers, seas

● Geography/environmental studies
Effects of water on land and different areas of the world
Water-tables (simple ones could be made by children) and the practical effects of erosion
Water related to weather – thunder storms, monsoon, tides, waves
Water and deserts
Tracing the routes of streams and rivers – from source to sea – and their stages of development

● Mathematics
Measuring – liquid containers
Volume and displacement – bowls, boats, ships
Size, shape – puddles of rain in playgrounds, locks, canals, seas, lakes or the sink and bath
Graphs – comparisons, measurement, volume
Movement – flow and volume

● Science
Mineral content – analysis
Animal, fish, insect and plant life
Aquaria in school
Studies of rushes and plants in rivers, aquaria, streams, ponds, seashore and lakes
Links with biology
Water creatures – drawing, photography and studies through microscopes

● Movement/dance/theatre
Moving to music after studying the movement of water and its rhythms
Study of water-flow from taps, hoses, fountains, streams, ripples on ponds, rain – splashes and drips

Swimming and floating
Movement of fish and water creatures
Films of movements of water, boats – sail boats and power boats
Translation of ideas into dance, movement, dramatic production, plays

Machines and mechanical movements

Machines provide a fascinating area for study, including 'moving parts' (mechanics of movement) which can usefully link a number of curricular areas. Children will need to have some mechanical parts of machines to look at, touch, draw and examine, for example:

    clockwork toys
    steam engines
    old sewing machines
    bicycles
    old motorbike parts
    clocks and watches
    electric shavers
    old kitchen implements
    typewriters

The intention is that one or more of these (or others which come to light) will be used in this project, a project embracing art, art history, mathematics, science and history. Here are some ideas:

● Art
Careful examination of the mechanical object (in total or in part), looking at machine parts and the way they work. The children could make drawings, rubbings, paintings and if a camera is to hand they could take photographs in black and white or colour.
Observational studies in pencil or ink and colour washes
Expressive and imaginative work – paintings and prints – of 'imaginary monster machines'
Collage patterns depicting movement – rotations or spirals
Work could be developed in three dimensions – sculptures made in card, wire, metal
Mobiles might be designed and made – depicting actual movement
Ceramics might be an interesting aspect to explore
Video films of machines in action
Pendulum painting machines might be used

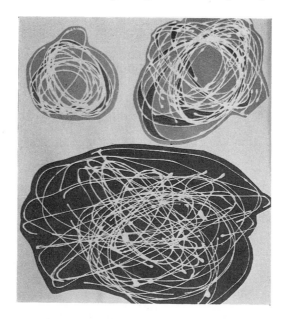

Plate 26 Pendulum painting machines are fun and they can be used for integrated work in art, science and mathematics. Simply fill a plastic bottle with watery paint or ink, suspend it on a length of fine string about three inches from the flat surface, and allow it to dribble onto a sheet of paper while at the same time rotating. The dribbled patterns may be coloured in with crayons and paints, or cut up and made into collage pictures.

- Art history
Studies of machines in an historical context – with an emphasis upon nineteenth and twentieth century industrialization. To include collections of illustrative material and visits to industrial museums, factories, local workshops and garages.

- Mathematics/science
Studies of simple mechanics, sources of power and conversions. Examination of the way gears operate.
Colliery winding gear, clocks, computers and other things might inspire studies of moving parts.
Use of plans, drawings, photographs, measurement and film. Development into reports, essays, model-making, etc.

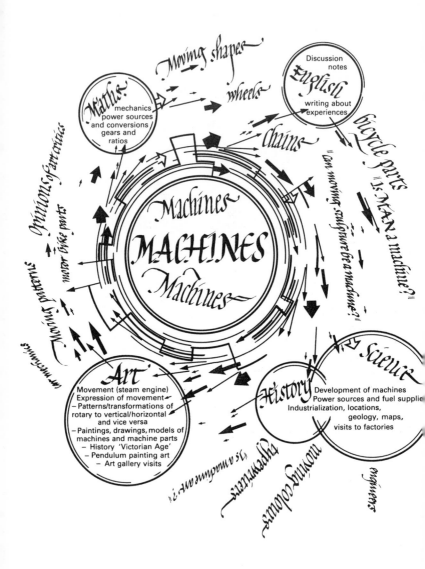

Figure 8 'Machines' — a topic idea. To examine the relationship between art, the machine and society, and to develop interrelated work using machines and machine parts as stimuli.

• History
Study of the historical development of machines.
Social implications of industry on society.
Inventions.
Effects of machines on developing countries as well as on the UK and USA.

It should be possible to integrate some or all of the curricular areas specified throughout a project concerned with this topic. Developments could include the inventive use of 3D materials and basic CDT tools (of a constructional kind). If equipment is available, video films might be made based upon 'movement in the machine'.

Snow

Like many other project themes this one is seasonal. Nevertheless, it can provide an exciting stimulus for interrelated work but will need to be grasped quickly when the occasion is there.

• Art
Studies of flakes of snow – falling, and on a window pane
Use of magnifying glasses or microscopes for observational sketches
Work could be developed into:
  • Paintings
  • Pattern work (in colour – crayons, paints, collage) or in (clay) or on (printed textiles)
Study of structures (related to mathematics/science)
Examination of colours in a snowy scene
Study of historical themes in art – medieval illuminated manuscripts, paintings by Breughel
Themes based upon snow-capped mountains and mountaineering
Photography and film-making

• History
Polar expeditions
Mountaineering
Links with medieval, Dutch and modern art

• English
Stories and poems about snow and winter
Descriptive work about actual scenes
Tape-recorders used to capture sounds
Work in drama
Tape recordings of people at work in the snow, playing in the snow – in

the playground, in the street, on the ski slopes, sledging, snow-balling, skating
The park – ducks on frozen ponds, people walking and running – studies of colours and snow
Film-making and closed circuit television (CCTV) productions

- Mathematics
Snowflake structures
Navigation
Tyre tracks and ski tracks, etc.

- Science
Study of polar regions
People, flora and animals in snowy regions
Temperatures
Icebergs – movement and flow, rate of melting, effects upon shipping routes
Ice on ponds, streams, water in school playgrounds
Studies of melting snow

An idea such as this can start off from a simple theme. As children get involved other ideas will be generated and groups will be activated into divergent thinking. Perhaps small groups will study different areas and cross subject boundaries as their work develops.

Trees

It is always surprising to realize just how many trees there are in the immediate environment. They are a constant source of wonder and provide an excellent source of study. The aim in this particular idea is to concentrate upon the identification of a small number of trees and to examine their patterns of growth, foliage, bark textures, life-cycles and ecology. Other objectives could be identified as project work and interests developed.

- Art
Collecting small branches, twigs, leaves, fruits, etc. for display and study
Observational drawings – in pencil, ink, ink and wash – of the objects (or parts of these)
Rubbings of the surface of bark
Photographs of the specimens and the trees

Display of leaves, twigs, pieces of bark, birds' nests and the observational studies
Developments might lead into painting, print-making, collage, three-dimensional models, ceramics in which a range of materials and techiques would be employed

- Mathematics
  Measurement – links with patterns of growth and natural structures
  Examination of the age of trees (circles of growth/cross-sections of trunk)
  Measurement of heights

- Architecture
  Use of wood in buildings (past and present), study of half-timbered buildings
  Consideration of structural and pattern qualities in timber constructions

- English/music/history
  Preparation of a symposium of poetry, prose and music
  Use of tapes of music, slides and films
  Reference to the shapes and forms of trees, colour, textures, pattern, historical facts and legends

- Science
  Selection of a single tree (or species of tree) for ecological study
  Include the study of birds, animals, lichens and insects

Further examination of woods would embrace the use of such material in past and present societies, the use of different trees – and reason for this – from all parts of the world. Studies of furniture design and making could be made, and the use of wood in weapons, transport, etc. considered.

The case for an art co-ordinator

Most schools do not co-ordinate their artwork and art activities but often appear to allow them to happen in a haphazard fashion. Surprisingly, this tends to work well, and if this is so then it might be wise to leave the process alone. Some schools have, occasionally, appointed one member of staff as a co-ordinator of art, giving him or her responsibility for the overall planning of the subject throughout the school. This can have advantages, for it means that someone who has a more specialist knowledge than other teachers in a school is in the position of an adviser, to whom teachers go for help and who can co-ordinate artistic efforts well, making them more worthwhile in an educative sense. Such a person could occasionally run brief practical courses in school for staff to give them experience of materials and new skills and to initiate ideas which are new to them. He or she might also move around the school to help in the practical teaching of the subject, and might be given responsibility for ordering art materials and controlling them within the school, as well as obtaining resource materials for general use. Displaying of work or other items could also be the responsibility of such a teacher and he or she might co-ordinate out-of-school visits to art galleries or the studios and workshops of artists and craftspeople.

The Education Reform Act 1988 establishes art as a 'foundation subject' (along with technology design) in the National Curriculum in Britain. The introduction of the National Curriculum into the primary schools might mean that they will need to consider appointing specialist art and craft teachers – perhaps specialist teachers in as many subjects as possible – in order to achieve good practice. This is certainly the view of the chief HMI for primary education. In a speech to the first national conference of the Assistant Masters and Mistresses Association (1988), he stressed that it was not realistic to expect primary class teachers to teach all subjects to the same high standard to mixed-ability, mixed-aged classes. In his view, subject consultants might be employed increasingly in the schools (Bayliss 1988: 12). The question of how schools obtain the services of specialists, where they will materialize from, and what monetary resources will be available to pay them with would, of course, have to be considered. Also, all specialists would require specialist materials and resources and these, too, would have to be provided. It is an interesting idea but an impracticable one in my view. I certainly cannot envisage it demanding any serious debate, for educational priorities lie elsewhere.

The value of collections of resource materials

It need hardly be said that collections of materials of all kinds are a very necessary aid to most forms of learning. This is particularly so in primary schools where children should be able to touch and handle objects. This arouses their inquisitiveness and permits them to make their own discoveries. What is more, if collections are readily available in the classroom or other parts of the school the children's immediate interest and questioning is catered for before it goes cold.

A school can be like a museum. It *is* a 'living' museum, not simply one which is seen behind glass panels, and resource materials are the keys which assist the teacher in unlocking many learning doors of discovery.

Note

Most LEAs have a School Loans Service containing all manner of original works of art, craft and design which schools may borrow. It might also include other items such as 'natural forms' — collections of shells, rocks, stuffed birds, bones, etc. — which are excellent aids for art and science studies, as well as video tapes and films. Headteachers normally hold catalogues or lists of items and will be only too pleased to help and encourage young teachers to obtain things from a centrally placed source in their area to encourage lively teaching.

5

Art in school

Art in the classroom environment

It must be remembered that children and their teachers spend a considerable part of their lives in classrooms. A classroom becomes almost like a second home and is a place in which the individual is identifiable within the larger context of the school. It is what might be termed a learning workshop in which children live, work, play and study and where it is possible for them to be relaxed and happy as well as engaging in concentrated and serious work periods.

Think back to the primary classrooms in which you spent such a large part of your own schooldays, and ask yourself the following questions. Were they interesting, or dull and boring places? Did they have pictures on their walls and objects on tables which could be touched? Were you excited and interested or were you dampened in your enthusiasm by 'schoolteacher' restrictions and material barrenness? The most crucial question of all should be will *your* classroom stimulate interest and a real desire to learn in the children you teach?

This final question is important, for each classroom reflects the interests of its teacher just as much as the interests of the pupils. The teacher sets the lead, sets standards, and orchestrates the learning environment. The classroom is a depository for 'things', objects of all shapes and sizes which children have discovered, in an attic, a junk yard, the street, a farm or play area – objects which have been brought in to be shared. These often become museum-like artefacts which make a classroom into a useful resource area containing a wealth of stimuli to learning. Old knarled roots or parts of trees can look like natural sculptures. Some may appear to be monsters and dragons with legs, heads, tails and horny skins. (see Plate 27) Could they, do you think, motiviate children to do imaginative work in clay? They might lend themselves well to being copied in paint and strong black and coloured felt-tipped pens. A strong light focused on to a natural wooden

Plate 27   Old knarled roots or parts of trees. Monsters or dragons? Such objects can be used in the classroom to motivate imaginative and creative work in several curriculum areas.

sculpture would create the most dramatic effect and might lead to the creation of set designs for classroom plays which the children invent and write themselves. Make room for one or two objects like this and you will provide yourself with an incredibly useful teaching–learning aid

83

Plate 28   Mirrored plastic sheeting (or ordinary aluminium foil) can be used to produce exciting visual effects from quite mundane objects.

which will inspire all manner of creative work in art, drama, mathematics, science and creative writing.

It is important to display objects in an exciting way so as to bring out their qualities and enhance their visual effect. Plate 28 shows what can be achieved by imaginative display of some quite mundane objects. Mirrored plastic sheeting draped from the classroom ceiling behind some ordinary objects produces the most incredible visual effects of distorted images. It seems to enhance colour and pattern effects so that children are presented with quite different visual stimuli for their art work. The most dramatic coloured and patterned effects can be achieved if, for instance, a green spotlight is directed on the objects from the left and a red spotlight directed upon them from the right. Children are then able to do observational paintings of (a) the objects and their images in the mirrored surface, (b) simply an area of 'distorted' images like that to the right-hand side of the photograph, or (c) they can apply more imagination to their art work in producing collages based upon distorted patterns and colours. (Mirrored plastic is not cheap but a similar kind of effect may be achieved with ordinary aluminum kitchen foil.)

A lively classroom abounding in interesting objects can help to promote good work, and in discussing school-practice preparation with my own postgraduate student-teachers I often stressed that the setting up and maintenance of a lively classroom demands energy, determination and care. It is possible to go into many classrooms which are just barren cubes containing regimented arrangements of desks or

Plate 29   Classrooms must be organized well if they are to function properly. Storage drawers can be neatly labelled, as here, to facilitate the learning operation with clear writing on white or coloured paper so that they look attractive.

85

tables as though straight out of the Dickensian era, and with children simply moping about unenthusiastically. A healthy classroom environment simply does not happen by chance but has to be planned and carefully monitored. It will have a profound influence upon children and its aim must be to stimulate them into meaningful activity.

It must be remembered that the more teachers and pupils put into the learning milieu, the more they will get from it. We are, after all, in the middle of a classroom revolution in which young people are encouraged to think and act for themselves. Gone are the days of 'chalk and talk', 'speak only when asked to do so' dictatorships, although it cannot be denied that such methods might be needed occasionally within the balanced framework of curriculum studies simply to steady a situation. But pupils now initiate and sustain much of their own learning in school. They learn how to develop ideas in depth because of their involvement in the learning process and, in consequence, learning is more meaningful to them. They are generally happy at school and want to be there in their youthful eagerness to learn.

A classroom in which art is an important learning tool is immediately apparent to the observer who walks in through the door. It throbs with visual excitement, an excitement evoked by creativeness which itself generates even more excitement, lively work and interest on the part of the children. Such a classroom will tend to have a healthy contagiousness about it and will be one which is a real stimulus to active learning. Displays of children's work will contain 'things' which the teacher and children have brought in. There will be an atmosphere of 'caring' and 'delight in beauty' which, in turn, will generate respect for natural and man-made objects, for the work classmates produce and, importantly, for the maintenance of order in the classroom environment – with materials and equipment looked after properly. The children will be allotted clearly-labelled storage facilities in which to keep their work so that they learn to be well organized and careful.

Using classroom space

As a multipurpose, learning workshop the primary classroom is not easy to organize and control; this calls for skill on the part of the teacher. Planning for activities in art – alongside the learning which is going on in other aspects of the curriculum – must be done sensibly, otherwise chaos may result.

Since the early 1980s, working groups of primary teachers in various

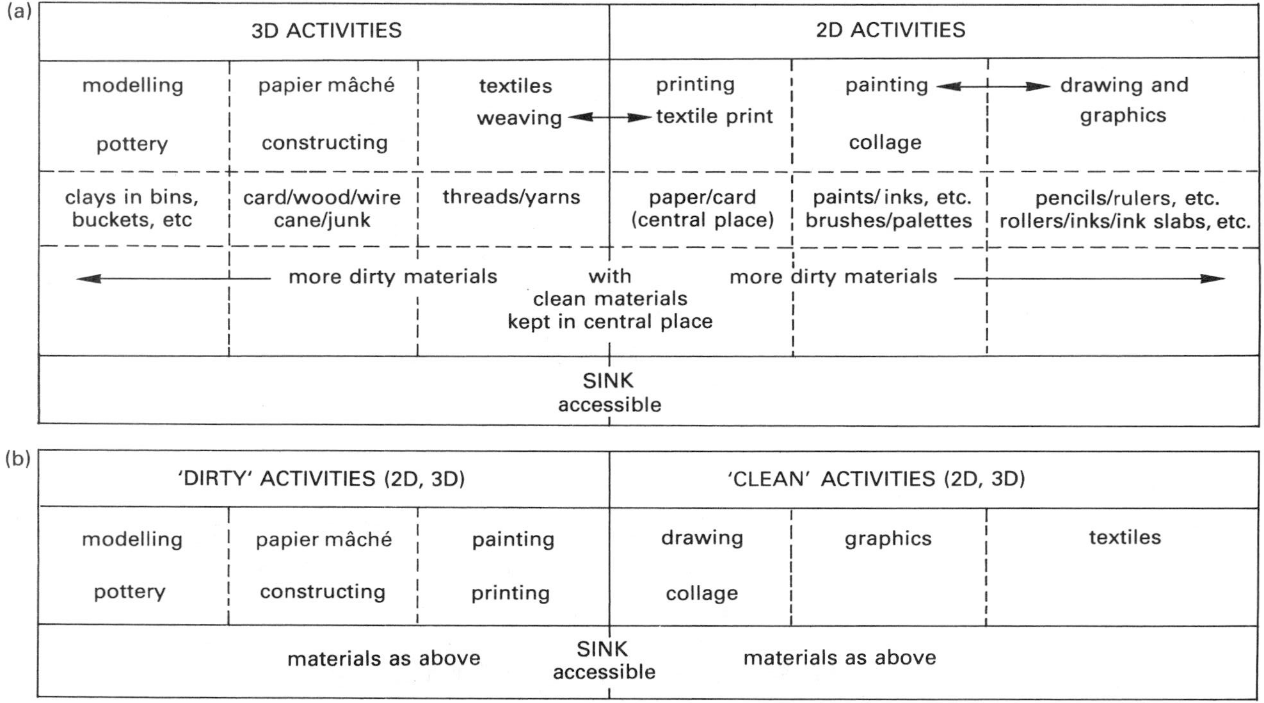

(a)

3D ACTIVITIES | | | **2D ACTIVITIES** |

modelling	papier mâché	textiles	printing	painting	drawing and
	constructing	weaving	textile print	collage	graphics
pottery					
clays in bins, buckets, etc	card/wood/wire cane/junk	threads/yarns	paper/card (central place)	paints/inks, etc. brushes/palettes	pencils/rulers, etc. rollers/inks/ink slabs, etc.

← more dirty materials — with clean materials kept in central place — more dirty materials →

SINK accessible

(b)

'DIRTY' ACTIVITIES (2D, 3D) | | | **'CLEAN' ACTIVITIES (2D, 3D)** |

modelling	papier mâché	painting	drawing	graphics	textiles
pottery	constructing	printing	collage		
materials as above			materials as above		

SINK accessible

Figure 9 (a) Art activities classroom plan; (b) Modified art activities plan.

LEAs have been studying this problem. In the mid-1980s one such group in Devon produced a diagrammatic plan which demonstrates how classroom space can be utilized for various art, craft and design activities (Lancaster 1987: 21). Its intention is that walls, cupboards, tables and shelves already available in the room should be juxtaposed sensibly so that resources are co-ordinated. 'Clean' materials (for drawing, painting, graphics, etc.) should be separated from 'dirty' materials (for claywork, etc.) for obvious reasons.

The art activities classroom plan (Figure 9a) consists of an area for 2D art work, and an area for 3D art work, with materials and tools available in each. In the modified version so-called 'dirty' and 'clean' activities are separated. Different situations, however, call for different strategies and what suits one classroom will not necessarily suit another. As an alternative way of working, a teacher might organize art into periods of activity so that 2D work is done for a period of time, followed by a period when 3D activities are engaged in. Common sense in the use of space and time is all-important, and it calls for 'good management' and 'good house-keeping'.

There is nothing so dull as a classroom that is static. Change is, in itself, a stimulus to children and new interests and excitements could be aroused simply by moving a cupboard sideways-on to a wall to create a small work area or resource centre.

Improvised room-dividers are easily made from sheets of hardboard, or from sheets of corrugated card which are pinned from ceiling to floor to provide effective temporary walls. If a room is dark, its walls can be lightened with paint or paper, or one or two small spotlights could be introduced to good effect. On the other hand, some classrooms benefit from the introduction of areas of colour. The permission of the headteacher should of course be sought before carrying out such alterations. You should also get in touch with the school caretaker, who may be able to help.

Teachers should think of their classes as effective three-dimensional spaces which they can alter. Discussions with headteachers and colleagues will provide some answers to problems, while visits to other schools will certainly help to engender change. An NSEAD publication listed a number of factors that teachers might consider and these are worth looking at:

- Are the work surfaces at the best possible height and are they of the most suitable material?
- Would it be helpful to cover them with hardboard or polythene?

- Could pupils move more easily about the room?
- Can obstructions such as cupboards be moved?
- Are the larger pieces of furniture, which divide up the spaces, providing the most useful floor areas?
- What are the main sources of light and are they free from glare?
- Can this be controlled adequately, e.g. with roller blinds or controlled lighting?
- Does the room provide for work areas of different character?
- Can these be provided in the room or are there better places elsewhere in the school to which children may go for special purposes?
- Could such work be suspended from the ceiling? It might be possible for specialist places to be provided in a school if teachers agree amongst themselves what each would be prepared to provide and for how many children. Practical craft and science facilities are often made available in this way by mutual agreement.

(Lancaster, ed. 1987, section 12)

As an artist I have always looked at a classroom space in the same way that I would look at a piece of sculpture. The classroom is an empty box into which I can slot other dimensional forms and, as such, it becomes a moveable sculpture which can occasionally be altered by myself or the children. Because this kind of change is possible, and therefore exciting, as the three-dimensional space within the box is altered it offers a strong visual and structural challenge which complements the art teaching which goes on in the classroom. The room, the teaching, and the learning mix naturally and are meaningful. In the past, and certainly from my own experience when I was in primary school, a classroom was a much more boring place, for very heavy iron and wooden desks stood in the same immovable rows year after year. Physical movement was curtailed in those kinds of classroom, and as a result creativity was also restricted.

An interesting design project which a junior-age class might find challenging would be one in which the children construct a four-sided box in card, with the top open. This open-topped box would represent the classroom and should therefore be made as a scale model with the positions of doors, windows and other physical elements indicated, either cut out or by paint. Using card models of furniture, sinks, cupboards and screens, the children could arrange and rearrange the model classroom, changing the concept behind it. They could draw plans of various arrangements and add written notes to complement them, stating reasons for change so that various models could be compared and the 'pros' and 'cons' analysed. If possible, the county schools' architect could be invited in to look at the display of completed project work in order to cast a professional eye over the children's efforts and to make an assessment of them.

Equipment, materials and storage

At primary level art equipment should be kept to a minimum. It should consist of simple apparatus consistent with the kind of work primary school children are capable of engaging in. There is no need for expensive items which would, in any case, demand the expertise of specialists, and special accommodation. It is far more important for children to learn to use their own hands so that they develop manual control and dexterity. These are the best tools of all.

Art materials and equipment might include:

- brushes – hog hair and water colour brushes of various sizes (to be stored away after working sessions in a clean state but readily accessible for further work).
- easels – these are normally provided in a school and are usually of the kind that can be folded up and stood in a cupboard or corner of the room. Wall-easels can be made fairly simply from pieces of hardboard or similar materials so that they hinge on to a wall, or are attached in some other way, to form a sloping surface.
- papers and card – consisting of a range of colours, sizes and shapes kept in suitable drawers and cupboards where they are easy to obtain before or during working sessions.
- wood, wire, cane and junk materials – could be kept in large cupboard boxes.
- clay – can be stored either dry or wet in suitable containers such as buckets or plastic bins.
- pottery wheel – in my view, a pottery wheel is not essential in primary schools, as hand-modelling, forming and building is far more suitable for young children; if available, however, they can be very useful.
- printing inks, rollers and inking-up slabs – must be kept clean and within easy reach in a printing area or where print work is undertaken.
- yarns and threads –can be kept in drawers, cupboards or boxes.
- drawing boards and clips – may be improvised from pieces of

hardboard, formica or even strong card and are best stored on end.
- plastic construction materials – usually in kit form, they are best stored in professionally supplied boxes or plastic containers.
- cardboard waste, old newspapers, old wallpaper books – should be readily available for both teachers and children in suitable storage facilities.
- drawing implements – pens, inks, pencils, crayons, etc., can be kept in boxes, drawers or, in some instances, in racks to ease counting and checking after lessons.

There are obviously other items which have not been mentioned here but which will need to be considered. What teachers must ensure, however, is that they teach children to have respect for materials and equipment no matter how small and cheap to buy and children should learn to leave working areas clean and tidy after using them, ready for other children who will be using them next. Respect for materials and art equipment must be inculcated from the first day a child starts his or her schooling.

If space is available in a classroom or school building, then teachers could share some larger items of equipment such as a pottery wheel (one in a school would be adequate), a kiln, a work-bench, buckets, and containers for work in plaster. Obviously, some aspects of art require a little more teacher knowledge and there is the danger of a situation arising in which a really enthusiastic teacher manages to acquire, at considerable cost, a pottery wheel and kiln only to leave after a year or so rendering the equipment redundant, if no other teacher is interested in using them. Much thought must therefore be given to the actual need for certain items and whether the money required for them could be better directed elsewhere.

Displaying work

It is important to display work well. Display ideas and techniques are touched on in Chapter 6, Exhibitions around the school (page 100). It should not be thrown up quickly or carelessly, but should be mounted and presented with care and respect. It is normal for some walls in primary classrooms already to have display boards attached to them, into which pins or staples will go easily. However, many teachers find such areas inadequate and like to extend the display facilities in their classrooms by utilizing the backs of cupboards, table-tops, window sills, and corner areas.

Plate 30   An interesting, well-designed display which invites closer inspection.

Simple display stands may be constructed from cardboard boxes – which local supermarkets or corner shops are usually only too eager to dispose of – and these may be painted or covered with coloured paper or material. Hollow structures can be produced from large boxes like these or from wooden strips and card, while some standing display units can be made with strips of corrugated card. Display and presentation ideas will be discussed in the next section. The importance of classroom display is that it is an extension of the children's working surface, indeed it is just another working surface or area – a valuable teaching–learning aid – which can affect what goes on in the classroom quite significantly. It is therefore something to be valued and used with discretion, to stimulate and enrich the teaching and learning which goes on.

I have always tried to display work or objects with care so that the overall effect is aesthetically pleasing. In doing this, I have therefore attempted to work as a professional display artist, arranging colours, two-dimensional pieces and three-dimensional objects like basic elements in a picture. A display is after all like a picture and should tell a story while exhibiting its wares well. After doing two or three displays, I then ask small teams of pupils to do this work, telling them that it is an extension of their art, craft, and design experiences. They are composing patterns, making aesthetically satisfying arrangements and really producing a most valuable art product which is larger in scale

Plate 31   A display done by reception class pupils with no help from their teacher.

than their normal work but which is also being shared more comprehensively and in a more meaningful way. As the children's displaying skills develop I find them eager to do more and instead of it becoming a laborious chore for me to constantly do the display and presentation which goes on in the classroom – as well as in many parts of the school – it can become a delight to see these lively and child-oriented areas of visual pleasure.

Assessment

As in other aspects of the primary curriculum, the teacher must be ready and able to assess work and pupil progress in art. This will be necessary at some 'key' stages, although there will be arguments *for* assessment in art and counter-arguments *against* the assessment of it. Some teachers will assess their pupils, including the marking of their work, one with the other – a natural and understandable procedure. However, it is much more constructive to assess the progress of individuals, using basic criteria as yardsticks. This will need to be done in relation to the testing of all children at the ages of seven and eleven which, as 'bench marks' of achievement, teachers will have to understand.

The DES has put forward a policy with respect to attainment targets and assessment arrangements in relation to key stages, which teachers should study. The policy is for teachers to assess children formally at or near the end of each key stage, i.e. at the ages of seven or eleven, when they will have to report the levels of attainment a pupil has reached (DES 1989: paras 3.11–3.18). In doing this, teachers may need to consider both formal assessments resulting from course work and, particularly at age eleven, also marking a number of standardized tasks. The major differences at age eleven from assessment made at seven would be: (a) the tasks set would be more complex; (b) there would be more profile components; (c) the profile components would be more subject-related. How this is achieved would need to be decided upon by national and local teacher/inspector committees meeting, working, and making recommendations which would be appropriate to children and the expectations of the National Curriculum.

A simple form of record card or record sheet may be useful. This might be in the form of a postcard (or similar but larger card), or a duplicated sheet (A4 size). A series of coloured cards or sheets would identify different children, or different groups, or could be used to identify different years. Individual teachers or the staff of a school or

ART ASPECTS EXPERIENCED RECORD	NAME				
	YEARS				
1. *Drawing*	1	2	3	4	Comments
experimental					
freehand drawing of natural forms					
freehand drawing of man-made forms					
careful, measured drawing					
designing					
2. *Picture-making*					
painting from scenes					
experimental work					
painting from imagination					
collage pictures					
3. *Pattern-making* with pencils, pens, etc.					
with repeat motifs					
freely					
with collage					
with textiles: tie-dye printing					
4. *Graphics* lettering					
making posters					
making books					
5. *Modelling* with clay figures					
pots					
plasticine					
papier mâché					
6. *Constructing* card models					
paper models					
wood models					
wire models					
7. *Aestheticism* (art historical, critical, social studies) visits to: art galleries					
artists' studios					
talks					
discussions					
writing about it					
reading about it					

Figure 10   Art activities experienced — a record.

even a group of schools – depending upon the LEA policy operating – will need to think through their proposed strategies carefully so that the record/assessment system which they adopt is a sound one.

The example of a record card given here was produced by a group of teachers in an LEA working party. It is intended to cover the whole of a pupil's period in a junior school from 7 to 11 years of age, although it could be adapted for use at the infant stage. The idea is that ticks are placed in the appropriate year columns each time the pupil works in a certain aspect of art. As the record progresses the teacher is then able to see, at a glance, those aspects which have been neglected or where the child requires experience in order to achieve a broad education in art.

Testing children in art at seven and eleven will not be easy, since the subject is so extensive. It will be vital to decide how this should be done across the whole range of art experiences, and this is where teachers will find the use of records invaluable as proof that the subject has been experienced and as to whether the individual child has had a sound, sequentially-structured aesthetic education during his or her primary years and is ready to move on to the next stage of learning in the secondary school. The NSEAD publication noted the following:

Children should be able to make significant choices from a basis of educated aesthetic judgements. Record-keeping is important, for both individuals and groups, within and beyond the school, to:

- ensure continuity and direction in the art, craft and design experiences planned both within these aspects and across the curriculum
- monitor individual and group progress and development
- facilitate evaluation of curriculum and lesson content
- facilitate future planning of the curriculum

It will be required for subsequent assessment of syllabuses in art, craft and design. In an assessment profile, we must be aware of pupil:

1 perception – the exploration and examination of the world through the medium of the senses
2 selection – the selection of aspects which are perceived and which stimulate us
3 recognition – the recognition of ideas, feelings and solutions which the stimulus generates
4 expression – the expression of the recognised responses in some appropriate form

5   materials and techniques – the development of each child's ability to handle an increasing range of materials with growing confidence and skill
6   Visual language – the knowledge of and ability to use the basic vocabulary of line, shape, colour, tone, texture, space and pattern from which pictures are made as well as an awareness of the way in which artists in our own and other cultures have used them.

(Lancaster 1987: sec.18)

Marking art work is an interesting, although occasionally controversial, area. It depends upon two fundamental elements, subjectivity, and objectivity, and these must be applied with discretion by the teacher who is in the position of making critical judgements. The classroom teacher is in fact in a strong position, for he or she is there when the children do their art work and can see it develop through the various stages to the finished piece. This observation is coupled with an experienced teaching eye and experienced, professional judgement which should encompass these criteria:

1   is the piece of art a 'good' or 'mediocre' product for a particular child?
2   did the child work hard in producing it, or were his/her efforts below normal?
3   do I like the work? (subjective judgement) *and* does the child like it?
4   has it been done skilfully? (objective judgement relating to craftsmanship, with the child articulating his/her ideas in material form)
5   has the child progressed artistically since producing his/her last work?
6   has the child discussed the work with understanding and aesthetic judgement?

If a teacher intends to mark a range of work done by a class of junior children this can be done in different ways. Here are two ways of marking thirty drawings.

Version A

1   Place the pile of thirty drawings on the floor.
2   Go through these fairly quickly placing them in two piles – one to the left and one to the right – putting the 'good' drawings 'A' – as

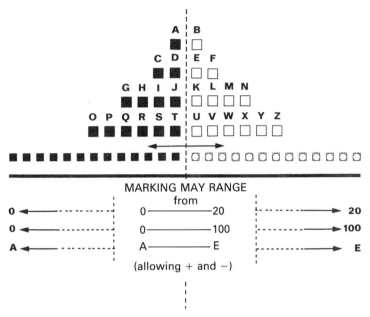

Figure 11   Marking children's work — version A.

they appear – on the left-hand pile and the others, 'B', on the right-hand pile.

3   Take the left-hand pile 'A' and repeat this process so that another two piles appear, 'C' and 'D', then do the same with pile 'B' so that two further piles of drawings 'E' and 'F' are obtained.

4   This process may be repeated a number of times depending upon the number of works being marked (see Figure 11).

This produces a spread of the drawings to which marks or grades may be allotted ranging from, say 1 to 20 and 1 to 100, or alternatively A to E – if grading of some kind is to be used.

Version B

This time the work is pinned up on a classroom wall with the best drawings placed in the top left-hand corner and the weakest in the bottom right-hand corner. These are arranged in horizontal rows, one above the other. This is a time-consuming method but it does allow the teacher to step back to review the work displayed from a distance.

Some years ago I was involved, along with almost fifty other teachers, in researching various methods of assessing art work done by young children. We employed at least six methods – working independently as individuals when no one else was around so that we were not influenced at all by what others had done – and when we came to analyse the results it was interesting that no matter what method was employed the marks were comparable in every case. Teachers may be assured that this will happen when they do their assessing.

Section 18, in *Art, Craft and Design in the Primary School* (Lancaster 1987) discusses evaluation and assessment, and one aspect which is stressed is the importance of continuous dialogue between teacher and child. This leads children to appraise their own work and to interpret the works of artists. (see DES, *The Curriculum from 5–16 1985*: paras 33–38). It gives them more responsibility and makes them increasingly aware of the value of self-assessment and self-criticism in what they do. This in turn teaches them to value their own opinions and not simply to accept the assessments and opinions of adults.

6

Art outside the classroom

Exhibitions around the school

Art has an important place in primary education. Through it we can try to cultivate in children a love for artistry and a feeling for beauty by means, in part, of practical work, but also through effective presentation. Personal discernment will be aided by experimentation with art materials, the use of art concepts, and the development of fundamental design criteria to make visual statements, and this will help children to develop craft skills and a more sensitive awareness of the world around them. It is a subject that can greatly affect the character of a school, for its products can be exhibited widely. In fact, art work is seen mainly through being exhibited.

When it is displayed with great care in school entrance halls, corridors, or in unexpected nooks and crannies, art work is automatically seen by children from every class, by their teachers, by parents, and by visitors to the school. As a visitor myself to many schools in this country, the United States, Africa and Scandinavia, I can say with certainty that the visitor gains a strong impression of a school's ethos when confronted by an exciting display of visual materials as he or she walks in through the door. Such a display sets the tone, and arouses interest and admiration through the high quality of what is on view. In my opinion art should pervade a school with a vibrating impact (Lancaster 1971b: 129–34). It can help enormously to give a school a cultural aesthetic that says, 'this is *this* school and no other'. An individual aesthetic which is strong gives a school a certain quality with which teachers and pupils can identify. It helps to weld the individuals in a school together with a sense of belonging and pride, for in it individual children are given recognition. Personal contributions are included for all to see and admire, and they are respected as essential elements in the learning syndrome.

Some items of equipment might be helpful to teachers responsible for mounting and presenting displays and these could be kept together as a display kit in a central point, such as the headteacher's room or the school secretary's office. It should contain pens, pencils, staplers and extra staples, possibly a staple gun (tacker), masking tape or sticky tape, dressmaker's pins (definitely not drawing pins, which are ugly and hinder rather than help display work), a cutting board, cutting knife, ruler, and scissors.

Some schools have a teacher, or small teams of teachers and/or children, with responsibility for general school displays. Others expect teachers to take turns in presenting exhibitions on a rotating basis. Whatever scheme operates, it is most important that careful thought be given to the planning and execution of display work, with the following borne in mind:

1 Content
   • a consideration of objects to be displayed
   • 2D objects only (pictures, patterns, photographs, etc.)
   • 3D objects only (pots, sculpture, puppets, shells, stones, flowers, plants, etc.)
   • children's work
   • natural objects
   • man-made objects
   • mixed work/objects, etc.
2 Location
   • is it right for the particular display?
   • is it the only place available?
   • will it be seen by those we wish it to catch?
3 Colour Scheme
   • a display is unified by a simple colour scheme; this will give it impact
   • consider different colour backgrounds black, black and white, red, green and blue, silver foil and yellow, or other schemes and combinations
   • use coloured card or paper for backgrounds
   • use drapes for backcloths
   • use corrugated card for backcloths and small stands
4 Background format
   • a well-considered, cohesive background to a display will be extremely helpful; once there it makes the rest of the display-work easy
   • background plain (one colour)

- background in vertical stripes (two colours)
- background containing a chequerboard arrangement of two colours
- a draped effect
- columns made from cardboard boxes (painted or covered with coloured paper, cloth or foil)
- open boxes used as display units

5 Lettering
- this should be selected carefully so that it is easy to read and gets a message across
- bold, clear titles (large pen or brush letters, letters cut out of coloured paper, Letraset letters, etc.)
- smaller notices containing information could be in script or type, but should be mounted on firm card

6 Lighting
- any display is brought to life by good lighting effects; if a school can afford some spotlights then these can be used with judicious effect, but if not, then one or two anglepoise-type lamps can be used
- highlight certain objects or works
- place lighting behind 3D objects to produce shadows and an exciting feeling of space and form
- introduce coloured bulbs

Varying depths can add a very useful three-dimensional effect to displayed objects. This might involve the combination of backgrounds (walls or display panels) and projections on tables or on the floor made from cardboard boxes covered with coloured card, paper or cloth. An effort should be made to create a stage-setting effect which will promote a feeling of wonder while stimulating questions. A display is, in fact, an extension of the working areas in classrooms. It is a focal point for enquiry, and as such is a vital component in education as much as books, videos or other teaching aids are (Lancaster 1987: section 19).

It is not difficult to come up with new suggestions for displays which will be useful to busy colleagues, for the education market is flooded with more ideas and published material than ever before. I have produced a short list, however, which can be adapted to suit various situations in schools, and these are based on ideas which have actually been tried out in schools:

Collections – natural forms

Rocks, shells, fossils, the bones of fish and small animals, flowers, twigs, and dried grasses are all suitable. These can be displayed and used independently or in suitably arranged groupings to form fascinating classroom 'resource' displays. Children can study such objects carefully, using magnifying glasses or even microscopes, and do careful drawings and paintings from observation. Such techniques have been used by artists throughout the ages, for they demand concentrated effort and help to develop very necessary art and design skills. Later, children might go on to develop some of their ideas in pattern making, painting, print making or even in textile design, pottery and sculpture. Yet again, they might make use of such classroom displays as a stimulus in their creative writing or the study of natural sciences and mathematical forms.

Collections of man-made objects

The list of suitable man-made objects is endless, and a small group of children would produce a large one within a few minutes. It might contain such 'found' things as rusty tin cans, old boots and shoes with their soles hanging off, collections of bottles, the mechanical parts of old clocks and watches, pistons and cog wheels, coloured plastic boxes, coins, stamps, workshop tools, worn-out tyres, etc. These and countless other items often evoke immense surprise and delight when they arrive some Monday morning or on a rather miserable winter's day and obviously they are a marvellous stimulation. They can quickly lead to the examination of structural forms, colours, pattern and the arrangement of shapes; and they can foster some very useful project work in art and related curricular activities such as mathematics, CDT, and so on.

Photographs, slides and films

These are invaluable to show children pictures of both natural and man-made forms which are just too large to bring into school but which might, nevertheless, be important to ongoing work. Photomicrographs, which enlarge the minutiae of nature – for instance the cellular structures of leaves, rocks, bones, a tiny part of a fly's wing which are invisible to the human eye – are invaluable if they can be obtained. They provide an enriching experience, as well as creating a feeling of awe and respect, and are extremely useful in supporting educational topics in nature study.

Educational toys and apparatus

These are in constant use in infant classrooms and much more use could be made of them in later years. Perhaps the best approach is for the teacher to place them around the room, as if casually, so that the pupils' inquisitiveness is aroused. They could focus on mathematics, geography, language, music, colour and light, living things, etc.; or simple scientific or mechanical experiments could be devised – often by interested children – with which pupils could experiment. Such things call for enquiring minds and encourage a great deal of discussion and self-education. Of course, it is possible to get older children to design and make their own educational apparatus – a process which involves them directly in thinking, making and doing: for instance, a science/art toy to teach some simple science and art concepts related, say, to cellular structures, pattern, colour, shapes and arrangements. This would relate art, science and mathematics in a worthwhile and interesting way.

Nature

Although we have touched briefly on this aspect in considering the classroom environment, it does not require much imagination to focus our eyes a little closer. How marvellous nature is. What scope it offers us.

We have probably all been on nature walks with our pupils, and what fascinating experiences these can be. The interest of a group of children – or even students and adults – can quickly be aroused on such occasions, for the madly-rushing world of today seems to drive us further and further away from the simple pleasures which nature provides. Remember the adage, 'stop the world for a moment and get off', Relax and enjoy it, and, surprisingly, learning will result.

Nature walks require some preliminary organization, of course, and classes or groups of children need to be prepared beforehand to make them really successful. Plastic bags, cardboard boxes or other containers must be provided by the teacher or the children themselves and these will be useful receptacles for 'found' things as they stroll in back alleys, parks, along hedgerows and river banks, or through woodland areas 'discovering' and 'collecting'. It never fails to amaze me that in a very short period of time the containers usually overflow with an abundance of bits and pieces – stones, rocks, broken red bricks, lichens, small plants, wild flowers, grasses of different species, feathers, leaves, pieces of bark, differently coloured sand and soil, insects, bits and pieces of rusty iron, and countless other items.

Back in school these need to be classified, arranged, mounted on card, carefully labelled and well-displayed. There is no need to teach, for this is a scientific or research exercise in itself and it provides many learning experiences. 'Discovery' sets the pace, and learning inevitably follows. This kind of 'going out' and 'display' learning is pupil-centred and although it is of an integrated form it is not just integrated for integration's sake. It embraces a number of aspects and calls for deep concentration, effort and disciplined response. Yet, as learning should be, it is enjoyable, it is real, it is fun and through its display it can be shared with others.

Encouraging work at home

Watching television tends to curtail children's inventive use of time in the home environment. It may be useful, nevertheless, for teachers to try to inspire their pupils to do some educational work away from school in their own time. This would be intended for the benefit of the children and should have the support of their parents.

If they have some art materials of their own they could be asked to do some drawing or painting. Even work in three dimensions is possible if waste materials are used, for this would not embarrass those children who could not afford expensive items. Studies of an artistic or craft kind would cost little if anything, for children could make quick sketches or notes in the locality they choose. They might draw in the street, in local shopping precincts, or in churchyards, and they could certainly be encouraged to make their own collection of 'things'. In requesting pupils to indulge in art (or other) activities which would complement the art studies which they do in school, teachers should try to ensure that they inform the parents. This would give them sound parental support and allay any possible antagonism.

In studying world art, design and architecture, the children should be encouraged to make use of the local library. Art books are usually expensive and beyond the pocket of many parents, but they can be borrowed for use at home or, alternatively, children could make study visits to reference sections in their library.

Art and design in the everyday world

Once children's visual education is extended, their perception of art in the environment will be sharper. Not only will children look out for the art

Plate 32 The façades of these buildings in the city of Bristol abound with geometric patterns and shapes which could be used as an inspiration for a range of art and craft work in the classroom. Here are some ideas: (a) standing structures made from strips of balsa wood, card and coloured cellophanes made to represent the buildings or as pure standing structures; (b) patterns based on repeated rectangles using sticky paper, crayon or paint collage; (c) prints, using lino and card strips, of the actual buildings. Skies and coloured textures could be added for effect.

around them, they will also look at what artists, architects, designers and craftspeople have provided for us in the way of visual imagery and articulated forms.

Project work could be based upon the idea of looking at and recording from the world around – in the street, in shops, in factories, in churches and even in the school itself – so that we increase their awareness. It is amazing how much art there is to be discovered. It will be seen in the street – in the form of lettering on shop fronts, on street signs, on posters and notices and painted on sides of vans and lorries; in the displays which abound in shop windows, where colour and arrangement are used; in the way pedestrians dress; in the design of cars; and in many other instances. Then what about the mass media? Many of us watch television daily, where moving imagery is colourful, and pattern, colour, and lettering are all utilized. We read magazines where the art of

Plate 33   This print was done by a top junior pupil who lives in an industrial area of a large city in the Midlands. He drew scenes and then interpreted them by using small scraps of hardboard (printed with the rough side so that a texture resulted), and printed railings with the edges of small pieces of card. The result is a bold and imaginative picture.

photography and typesetting is plentiful and juxtaposed by professional designers to give us articulated visual imagery.

I hope that enough has been said to encourage a concern for the everyday aspects of life and the richness of material it offers. Children will discover an abundance of interesting things of tremendous value to an education in art, and the wise teacher will tap this resource unremittingly.

107

Plate 34 'Bicycles'. If we take the trouble to look through the wheels of bicyles like these in the school cycle shed we are immediately into the realms of mathematics and engineering. This subject would pose quite complicated problems for children to solve if they took it as a topic for drawing, painting, collage or sculpture. They would have to think hard about the methods to be used and the materials which would be appropriate for their work.

Using art galleries

Visits away from the day-to-day environment of school are always a stimulus to children's learning. They are a change from mundane classroom studies. Children are excited by them and are often much more willing to ask questions, to study, and to learn from them.

Local art galleries are most useful teaching aids and should be used as such. To maximize their learning potential visits should be planned and organized well, for they will simply be time-filling, time-wasting exercises if no preplanning has taken place. Children require some structured guidance on visits, perhaps originating from the work they are doing in school. Duplicated question sheets with answer pads and writing implements might assist them in this. Question and answer approaches will focus attention and enquiry upon relevant issues or works

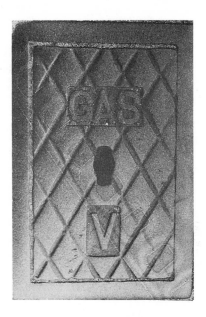

Plate 35   Interesting objects abound in our daily environment. A metal cover like this one contains a pattern and bold sans serif letters. Children might make rubbings of it with black or coloured wax on paper, learning more about texture and shape.

of art. Some works, paintings, sculptures, or textiles, for example, might be preselected for study, to fit into a topic or to illustrate points of relevance to classroom work. Such planning will maximize a visit, avoiding a situation in which individual children flit aimlessly around a gallery using it as a playground. When this occurs we can be sure that the teacher has been careless or lazy in his or her preplanning.

Many galleries will offer invaluable help to schools in the organizing and structure of visits. They invariably employ specialist education staff who are experienced in coping with this and with groups of visiting children, and they will usually be very willing to co-operate with programmes of work which may be started in the gallery and then completed back in school. Gallery resources are in various forms. There are usually original pictures (oil paintings by great artists, pictures by water-colourists, paintings in acrylic materials by modern artists), prints (etchings, aquatints, lithographs, etc.), sculptures (in bronze, wood, stone, resins, etc.), and possibly some examples of pottery and textiles. Works will be catalogued – these are often useful aids for children's project work – and they may have postcard reproductions, slides, leaflets, and booklets which it is possible to purchase. Art gallery resources are there to be used. Some galleries also provide a helpful loan service and are often willing to allow their staff to visit schools to talk about visits or to conduct projects. They might have artist-fellows who would also be pleased to show children what they are doing and to discuss their work with them. People like this may be able to attach themselves to a school for short periods as 'artists in residence', and teachers should make enquiries if they would like to encourage this idea.

Artists in residence

Some LEAs – or even individual schools – run an 'artist in residence' scheme in which artists and craftspersons participate. A painter, a potter, or a sculptor will, for instance, work in a school for a period of time (which might be one day each week for a number of weeks, or for a concentrated period of two or three days), using a classroom or available area of space as a kind of studio/workshop. This gives the children the opportunity to see adult artists at work and even to work alongside them which, in a sense, is akin to the old 'master/apprentice' situation when the novice worked alongside the skilled practitioner to learn a craft or trade so that he or she could see what was involved in the 'making' situation and participate increasingly in it. It is good for schoolchildren to meet practising artists and craftspeople, and it is even better if they can do so in their own schools. Two or three concentrated periods of interaction are an enormous stimulus, and can initiate pupil involvement with materials which might otherwise escape them.

If teachers wish to plan this kind of operation they might:

- contact their own Art Adviser
- make enquiries at their local teacher's centre
- ask for help from local art/craft organizations – some of which might have excellent amateur artists in their ranks
- know of local craftspersons (basket weaver, blacksmith, potter, weaver, silversmith, textile designer, and so on) who might be willing to give some time to such an enterprise
- approach a nearby high school where fifth or sixth form students might be keen to offer their services

• seek help from a local art college or technical college

Teachers would need to plan the organization of artist in residence periods with care so that they would be assured of success, and might be wise to ask:

• is the artist or craftsperson a 'pure' artist who knows nothing at all about teaching? If so, then a teacher, or teachers, might need to be aware that he/she will need some assistance occasionally
• 'pure' artist/craftsperson contact with children can be extremely exciting and beneficial. However, there may be occasions when the artist's lack of pedagogical knowledge and/or experience could, in fact, be detrimental, and if this appears to be the case then some subtle yet skilful guidance from a teacher might be necessary so that the workshop experience is not a wasted one
• is it sufficient for an artist in residence (a sculptor, for instance) to work at his or her three-dimensional work for a period of, say, three days and to have no contact with, or not to talk about the work to, the children? The teacher and artist might think that it is
• should the artist, on the other hand, encourage children to express themselves in some way with similar materials?
• if the children are encouraged to work alongside the artist should they simply be left alone with materials so that they can express themselves freely, or be given some directions and guidance?

The artist/craftsperson in residence immediately places himself or herself in the position of being an 'educator' – the very presence of such a person ensures this. He or she must, therefore, have specific reasons for whatever is done, and before commencing the period of residence in a school ought to think about the reasons for taking certain actions – questioning these and even analysing them. It is up to the teachers concerned to ensure that an exercise of this kind is undertaken seriously and with considerable thought. I can assure you that when it is, the experience will be an enrichment both of school life and of the children's aesthetic education and that it is well worth the effort and time devoted to it.

7

Some ideas

A painting scheme for top juniors

This painting scheme has been set out here as a series of sequentially considered lessons, although it is appreciated that it is not always possible to pursue art work in the primary school in this way. Teachers might wish to consider each lesson as a stage or possible direction in which children might move. What is important is that individual teachers should employ a degree of flexibility and plan what they do according to the needs of their pupils, and what they have experienced previously.

Materials and equipment needed

Paper, card, paint, 'found' paints (these are the home-made variety which result from experimentation with mud, cold tea, coffee, beetroot, dyes, etc.), brushes, paint spreaders (palette knives and/or improvised paint spreaders – card or kitchen knives or pieces of wood, etc.). Easels, boards, clips are useful but not essential. Coloured photographs and/or slides of the work of two or three artists can be used.

General aim

The following scheme of six lessons (or stages) is intended to give the children sequentially structured experiences in painting so that they enjoy using paint, do a variety of interesting things with it through experimentation and self-discovery, and employ some or all of their newly-discovered painterly experiences and associated skills in the production of a well-considered painting – the outcome of a period of sustained hard work and motivation. They should also be encouraged to relate their work to that of more experienced artists.

Specific aims

1 to get the children to experience and understand different constituencies of paint and different paint qualities, i.e. 'thick', 'thin', 'washes', etc.
2 to let the children discover for themselves the joy of mixing paints and of experimenting with different painting techniques, with the specific intention that they should develop their own 'painterly' techniques of working
3 to develop their expertise in, and as a result, their knowledge of, colour-mixing and the handling of thick paint
4 to get them to explore paint 'textures' by means of a demonstration by the teacher, discussion, and further experimentation with paint. They might also do so by copying surface textures on a shell, a piece of bark, and so on
5 to get the children to extend their experimentation and develop skills further in the production of a well-considered painting (a still life, a landscape, etc. – possibly recorded direct by sketchbook-type drawings)
6 to bring the children to a critical evalution of their work by means of a display of it, a discussion of what they have done and achieved (i.e. how successful they have been), and a discussion of the work of two or three mature artists.

Lesson 1: exploring paint

Children should be encouraged to explore its nature, its possibilities – thin, thick, applied with fingers, rags, brushes, etc.

- thin washes of paint are mixed then flooded on to a sheet of paper with a large brush, screwed-up dampened ball of newspaper, or a small rag
- after allowing the sheets to dry, thick colour could be applied in some areas
- textures can be explored – wax crayon marks made and further washes applied in some areas
- drawings in ink can be done over some parts of the dried washes or textured areas

Lesson 2: making textures

Exploring textures of all kinds using the maxim that 'texture refers specifically to the quality of a surface – either the visual quality or the tactile quality' is a useful experience for young artists. (This is essentially a 'painting' exercise.)

- in order to develop 'painterliness' this lesson will be devoted to doing 'thick' textures, so the children will mix small quantities of very thick paint
- using a small brush and thick paint, children can make small areas of textures (say at least eight different ones to each child)
- a match stick or pin head could be used instead of a brush
- some textures can be added to more than once to build up textured effects

Lesson 3: colour mixing

- the relationship between the three primary colours can be explored
- adding white to a mixed colour can be seen to give it body
- adding colour to colour can be experimented with
- children can try adding black to a colour or mixed colours
- it is important for children to mix colours, not simply to use ready-mixed paint straight from a pot. In mixing colours they will learn what happens when two or more colours are mixed together, which is an exciting and educational thing to do
- they could commence by experimenting freely to see for themselves what happens and how many different colours they can obtain
- later, a more formal approach might be sensible and they could simply mix red and blue/yellow and blue/yellow and red, concentrating upon the three primary colours only
- the addition of some white paint to red, then yellow, then blue will be interesting
- they could go on to do the same with green, orange, and violet
- touches of black to white, red, then yellow will produce different effects as, indeed, it will to other colours
- each pupil might produce a colour chart, or a group of children could do so together

Prints or slides of artists' work will be extremely helpful in making points about the use of colour in art – sombre, lively, bright, happy, etc.

Lesson 4: drawing the subject

- draw, with a brush and thick colour (not with a pencil), direct from a still-life group, a person (say, draped in a costume), some flowers, with strong, bold brush strokes
- using this technique look at sketches which have been done in sketchbooks of a landscape, trees, ships in the docks, etc.
- using this technique consider imaginative subjects such as 'insects', 'space flights', 'space wars', 'under the sea', etc.
- use the bold, brush drawings as a guide and complete the painting with 'thick' paint and textures (this painting might even take two lessons)

Lesson 5: completing the painting and mounting it on paper or card

- as it is important that the painting should be 'painterly' and done with care it would be wise to insist that *two* lessons be used
- part of this lesson could be devoted to the mounting of the painting on paper or card

Lesson 6: display/evaluation/discussion

- careful display of the work produced
- assessment of what the children have done – both by the teacher and the children – and how successful they have been
- discussion of their work in relation to the work of two or three artists (using coloured prints or slides)
- consideration of other ways of working (for possible development in future schemes)

    could they use charcoal as an alternative way of starting a painting off?

    what about shadows?

    could thick paint be applied with a brush better than, say, a palette knife?

    as such knives are expensive it might not be feasible to use them in a junior school; however, plastic knives are cheap, as is card, and both can be used very effectively

    using thick textures and looking at objects, landscapes, etc., will make the children 'look' differently and with a keener eye

At the end of lessons it is sometimes helpful if the children's work is placed on the floor so that everyone can see what has been done. This will give each pupil a chance to say something about the painting or texture/colour experimentation.

It might be interesting to arrange to have some prints of one or more artists' work which have been discussed alongside the final display of the childrens' work. Also, the children might find it interesting to write

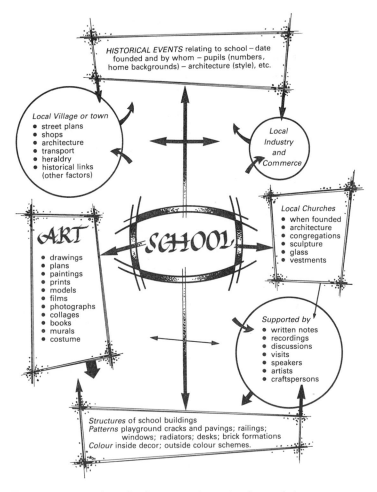

Figure 12 Using the 'school' as a starting point for work in art or as an integrated project idea.

some brief notes about what they did, and these could be added to the display.

Using 'the school' as a starting point for work in art and/or as an integrated project idea

Children are in school for five days every week, and usually think of school as a work place. So it is and so it should be. However, it is sometimes helpful to look at it in a different way, for its environment is full of useful stimuli for all manner of learning. It can offer starting points for visual work in art or to initiate integrated projects. This chart is self-explanatory. It is given simply as a guide and to stimulate some thoughts. Once the teacher has decided upon an idea such as this one, a quickly-sketched plan can be helpful and even expanded upon when work is underway.

A school newspaper (an integrated project)

This idea may appear rather a mudane one for children to engage in, yet it should provide opportunities for them to work as designers, reporters, editors, organizers, co-ordinators, possibly typists, layout and paste-up artists, interviewers, and distributors so that they develop a variety of skills and techniques in a realistic and meaningful fashion.

If a school decides to run a newspaper then children from every class can be involved both as permanent and occasional newspaper staff. This does not mean that they 'down tools' and pour all their efforts into its production, rather that the more permanent ('editorial' staff) keep it ticking over each week with individuals and small groups injecting ideas and materials as and when these are required. The idea will need to be discussed and planned thoroughly if it is to be successful, and a workable procedure will need to be adopted.

Planning

An editorial team must be formed, who should consider the following:
- the number required
- what their task will be
- who the newspaper will be aimed at
- how it will be designed

- what its contents will be
- how it will be produced
- how many copies will be produced
- will it be a 'free' newspaper or will it be 'for sale' so that costs will be covered?
- what size and shape it will be
- other considerations which occur in individual situations

A school I know of ran such an enterprise most successfully for a period of almost two years. A weekly edition of 200 copies was produced and the majority of these were sold to school governors, teachers, parents and some to local traders so that production costs were adequately covered and some money remained for the school fund. It consisted simply of three double-sided A4 pages.

Production

A production team might comprise an editor, reporters, designers/layout artists and would be responsible for:

- designing each edition after a 'house style' had been decided upon
- putting together all the editorial material – copy, illustrations, drawings, photographs, advertisements, etc., and pasting up such material ready for printing
- designing suitable advertising for the newspaper

Obviously, a newspaper must contain a range of interesting items. These might include news, school interests, class interests, individual interests, sport and the like, but the editorial staff would sift the materials carefully and decide which of these should be included in any edition.

Editorial and production teams will obviously be restricted by existing facilities and costs of materials, but as most schools possess a typewriter – if not, a second-hand machine can be obtained quite cheaply – and copying machines, neither of which will be in constant use, they should activate projects quite reasonably. Hand-written copy could be juxtaposed with typescript to give visual variety.

Having initiated the idea it will be possible for a planning team to design an overall format as well as a page layout (with columns, spaces for art work and illustrations), and with bold, legible titles (sometimes done with printed letters cut from potatoes). A 'master layout sheet' might be helpful so that weekly layout design is made easier, and this can be helped if a number of photocopied sheets are printed on which copy, titles and illustrative materials are pasted in readiness for copying.

Where can such an enterprise be undertaken? Well, I have seen little-used corners in school halls, corridors and even classrooms adapted well. A table or desk will be necessary in such a production base with, if possible, an area of wall (or a soft board background), on whose surface material can be pinned or taped by 'reporters', and by 'production' and 'artist/layout' staff when they have collected this together.

A newspaper will need to be distributed, and another small team could be given this responsibility.

Simple print-making

This scheme of simple, practical art lessons can be adapted quite easily by the primary teacher to either the infant or junior stages. The main idea behind it is to introduce children to some basic print-making techniques and, through a few ideas, to stimulate them to go on to develop graphic imagery further.

Materials required

- water-based printing inks (black, white and the three primary colours) – paints might work well as a substitute
- inking-up slabs (small pieces of card, 4–6in/10–15cm or pieces of formica)
- one or two inking-up rollers (2in/5cm or 3in/7.5 cm rubber-coated rollers)
- brushes
- a variety of papers (black, white and coloured)

Printing with found objects

- small sticks, stones, pebbles, leaves, bones, shells, etc.
- ink-up an object and print marks from it on to a sheet of paper in one colour
- repeat this operation with two or more colours
- go on to produce 'textured' images
- develop the idea further to give 'multiple' images

Some ideas

Printing with 'man-made' objects

- pieces of rubber (tyres, soles of shoes, etc.), pieces of string, wire, net curtain material, crumpled paper, kitchen foil, machine parts (from clocks, watches, other machines)
- go through the stages experienced in 'printing with found objects' above

Developing printing further

- composing pictures using a mixture of natural and man-made printing objects (landscapes, faces, people, animals, space pictures, etc.)

Prints from vegetables

- slice through vegetables (a potato, a carrot, a swede, a cabbage, etc.) and print one or more images
- develop this into multiple image pictures or patterns
- a cob of corn inked-up and rolled will give some interesting effects
- add brushed-on colours and/or drawn ink lines, textures and shapes

Paper prints

When using this type of printing cut or torn paper shapes are used as basic printing blocks to produce:

- single images
- double images
- multiple images
- repeated images
- images of letters
- landscape pictures

Card prints

- cut or torn card shapes may be used in much the same way as paper was used to make paper prints above

Plaster prints

Plaster blocks may be employed as printing blocks:

- their surfaces may be printed from direct, having been inked-up first
- tools of various kinds may be used to produce incised marks in the surfaces of the blocks with nails, saws, knives, chisels, etc.
- specific shapes may be carved into the blocks – i.e. letters, pictures of trees, houses, people

Lino prints

Pieces of lino (1 in/2.5 cm square, or larger) may be cut into with sharp cutters, inked-up and prints taken from them. Here are some treatments:

- hammer marks (made with a hammer or a chisel)
- hammered patterns (made with a nail and a hammer)
- cut marks (using a saw)
- patterns or pictures made by using lino cutters
- two-colour prints (using one or more of the above techniques)
- multi-coloured prints (using any combinations)

Wood grain prints

These prints are simply taken from pieces of wood with pronounced graining:

- rubbings (black wax on white or coloured papers)
- rubbings (white wax on white paper with thin washes of black ink brushed over)

String prints

To produce string prints a block is used comprising a piece of strong card, hardboard or wood on to which is glued some pieces of string:

- straight lines to produce linear patterns and repeating patterns
- straight line pictures (trees, mountains, aeroplanes, people, etc.)
- wavy lines (patterns or seascapes)
- zig-zags
- spirals
- curved lines
- trees
- wavy grass
- curved lines

Some ideas

Monoprints

A monoprint is produced by:

1   inking-up an inking-up slab (this could be a sheet of paper, card, hardboard, formica or glass) with black or coloured inks – use a roller to do this
2   placing a sheet of paper face-down on the inked-up slab
3   drawing with a pencil, ball-point pen or other pointed implement on the paper
4   peeling-off the paper carefully to reveal the inked pattern or picture underneath
5   allowing the 'monoprint' to dry
6   adding more colour with a brush (if desired)

Slightly more complicated shapes may result if cut or torn paper shapes are placed on the inked-up slab to blot out areas of colour before the paper is laid on it. Other printed areas or colour/texture/pattern may be added by using other print methods already discussed.

Polymer 'dribbled' prints

Blocks may be made by dribbling polymer paint on to pieces of strong card, hardboard or wood. These are then used as printing blocks much as 'string' prints were produced.

Line prints

It is possible to make some very interesting simple, or complicated, line prints by using the edges of card, wood, or even metal to produce them.

• ink-up the edges of pieces of card (with a brush or roller) and print straight lines with these
• repeat this with wooden strips or metal strips
• produce prints of two, three or more colours
• go on to do some over-printing
• images may be developed if tin lids are inked-up and printed

Four starting points

These four ideas might be helpful as the basis for creative art work. They could be developed in different ways, depending upon the interest of pupils and the materials available.

1   You will need a collection of *stones and rocks* of various shapes, sizes and colours:

- pick up one of the stones and feel its surface
- look very carefully at this stone, considering its form
- make a drawing of the stone (using a pencil, biro or fibre-tipped pen)
- take three or four stones and place them together in a group
- draw this group
- arrange more stones together on a sheet of coloured board, card or paper and make a 'rocky-landscape painting' using the group as a stimulus
- add some strong clouds to the sky area and three knights in armour riding across the landscape

2   Collect some bottles of various sizes and colours

- draw the shapes of some of the bottles on paper of different colours – these need not be to scale
- cut out these coloured bottle shapes and then arrange them on another sheet of paper to form a collage pattern
- overlap some of the bottle shapes
- if you feel very creative set up a row of bottles and get someone to look at you; make a transparency picture (this will be like a stained glass window) based upon the impression of the face seen through the coloured bottles and the bottles themselves

3   Look inside and outside the school building for a variety of textured surfaces;
- use wax crayons to make a series of 'rubbings'
- cut these into a number of pieces and use them to produce a circular pattern
- add some areas of thick paint with a small brush or the end of a tiny stick to add other textured effects

4   Select a plant or flower:
- make a drawing of part of it
- use some three-dimensional materials (paper, card, foil, and wire), and construct a plant-like structure based upon the drawing you have made
- you can be quite inventive and need not worry about your plant structure looking real
- add coloured cellophanes or paint to give your 'sculpture' more interest

8

Project work based upon heraldry

Heraldry would seem to be an ideal medium to inspire art, craft and design work which will fire young children's imagination. Even if they don't understand it they can at least enjoy its use of decorative patterns, images and colours. Heraldry appeals to the imagination in a 'romantic' sense, although it was originally associated with wars and knights. It provides a fascinating historical study which embraces kings, queens, early barons and war lords in medieval times, right through to the present day when it is also used by individuals, local Boroughs, corporate bodies, educational institutions, industry, and, of course, by the armed services.

In the Middle Ages people recognized the *visual imagery* associated with their feudal lords. They would know their shields of arms and close retainers would wear lord's badges on their tunics. Today's population are better educated and are able to read, but our pupils also rely on visual imagery and can still learn much from studying local heraldry and how it came to be designed. Indeed, they are able to draw or photograph examples on buses and municipal buildings, or they might make coloured sketches of heraldic achievements on carved monuments in local cathedrals and churches.

Church heraldry itself can be a fascinating subject for study. Ecclesiastical armorial bearings are similar to those of laypeople, but there are differences which make them interesting and unique. Some of this can be seen in books dealing with the manuscripts which scribes produced in medieval monasteries and abbeys, but a great deal of information and help may be forthcoming from cathedral authorities who would probably be delighted to offer help.

An aspect of this subject which has great appeal is 'flags'. There are a number of different types all of which will arouse and sustain interest which has educational value, and learning about the reasons for their design and use could lead to some valuable research.

When I was teaching children I occasionally involved my classes with heraldic projects which related to aspects of design, pattern and colour

Project work based upon heraldry

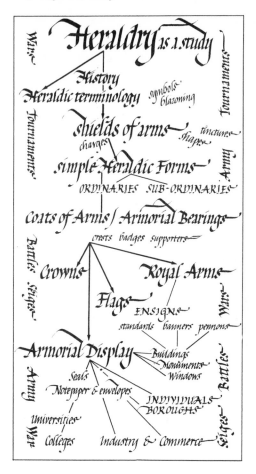

Figure 13   Project work based on heraldry inspires an endless variety of ideas.

relationships which we were studying in general art lessons. In no time at all the classroom vibrated with colourful displays of shields, flags and pictures of knights. What is more, it was a tremendous stimulus at Christmas time (when we were responsible for decorating the school halls and corridors), providing endless resource material.

Heraldry is a pictorial science. Certain rules must be adhered to so that there is 'correctness' and 'consistency', then at a later stage children can be encouraged to experiment and to carry their ideas further in an inventive manner.

Some ideas for projects on heraldry

The chart 'heraldry as a study' contains a range of ideas which could be used as possible themes. It would be silly to attempt too much, but over the course of two or three school years the pursuit of a number of projects would help the young pupil to build up a considerable knowledge and experience of the subject. He or she would also be encouraged to read more about heraldry and to be much more aware of its existence in the most unexpected places, where it adds colour and decoration which is effective and aesthetically pleasing.

1   The history of heraldry
   ● written and illustrated studies of the development of heraldry
   ● its origins in the Holy Land – the 'Crusades'
   ● social prerequisites for the creation of heraldry
   ● heraldry in warfare
   ● feudal armory – lords (masters) and servants in the medieval world
2   Armorial knowledge
True and authentic heraldry depends upon a complex armorial knowledge and art. It is governed by rules which are laid down by the heralds at the College of Arms, and studying these could form the basis for a project:
   ● terminology
   ● symbols
   ● tinctures
   ● forms (Ordinaries and Sub-Ordinaries)
   ● charges
   ● heraldic beasts
3   Designing and making shields of arms
   ● various shapes, which have changed over the ages
   ● display in rows and in groups
   ● use in classroom drama
   ● conventional designs as well as new ideas and concepts
4   Crests and badges
   ● coloured drawings of crests
   ● depiction in three-dimensional form to be worn on helmets
   ● study of historical examples in books

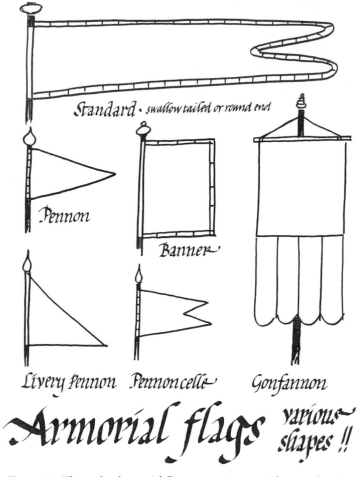

Figure 14   The study of armorial flags arouses interest with great educational value.

 • design of a school badge, a team badge or a class badge
5   Crowns
There are a number of different crowns and children find that they discover much which will interest them if they explore this topic.

 • drawings in pencil, ink, colour

- models in card, fabric, metal
- variations and developments concerned with coronets (Duke/Marquis/Earl/Baron, etc.)
- ancient crowns and others, to be researched

6   Flags

Standards – ensigns of war

Pennions – personal ensigns of knights

Banners

National Banners – the flags of countries, ensigns, military flags

- historical studies
- art/design work in printmaking/textiles/embroidery
- different shapes depending upon rank and usage

7   The lion in heraldry

Local studies will be enhanced by fieldwork. Children could visit local churches to see monuments and stained glass windows. They will find various heraldic interpretation on pub signs – some of which are quite splendid in conception, design and execution. Historic houses, too, often provide a feast of heraldry, while a walk down the main street in the nearby town will throw up some surprising discoveries.

Recently I visited the battle field of Crêcy – where ancestors of mine (de Lancastre knights from Westmorland, now called Cumbria, and Lancashire) fought – and my imagination ran riot. Masses of knights in armour with their colourful shields, lances and swords; horses coated in armour and covered with armorial drapery; archers firing thousands of arrows; screams and shouts as charges were made and combat ensued – what a subject for painting, drawing, print-making and model-making.

The subject of heraldry is an excellent one for cross-curricular studies. Ideas are plentiful and teachers need only use a small amount of imagination in order to stimulate their thinking and planning. It has a fascination which can capture a child's imagination and lead to a lifetime's interest, while providing a springboard for work which is invaluable in an educational sense.

9

Two case studies

The art and design problems outlined in this section are used to illustrate two developmental curriculum projects undertaken in primary schools. Their objectives, the environmental backgrounds and the teacher–pupil interests varied, although these factors have not been emphasized or allowed to predominate. It is hoped that teachers will use the studies for comparative purposes or to help in stimulating other ideas. In this sense, they are simply presented as catalysts in the hope that children in schools will benefit.

Any curriculum activity must be suitable as a learning experience for children and will require careful consideration and planning:

> bare doing, no matter how active, is not enough. An activity or project must, of course, be within the range of the experience of pupils and connected with their needs – which is very far from being identical with any likes or dislikes which they can consciously express. This negative condition having been met, the test of a good project is whether it is sufficiently full and complex to demand a variety of responses from different children and permit each to go at it and make his contribution in a way which is characteristic of himself. The further test or mark of a good activity, educationally speaking, is that it have a sufficiently long life-span so that a series of endeavours and explorations are involved in it, and included in such a way that each step opens up a new field, raises new questions, arouses a demand for further knowledge, and suggests what to do next on the basis of what has been accomplished and the knowledge thereby gained.
>
> (Skilbeck 1970: 45)

I feel that the case studies given here were excellent learning experiences which embraced the criteria above. The teachers concerned had an understanding of the nature of learning and how children respond.

Case study 1

The visual qualities of the daily environment offer children a major source of reference, for in their school work they can draw from their surroundings with relative ease. Children do not have to rely exclusively upon the expressive potential of art materials or spontaneous improvisation of unobserved shapes, forms, colours and textures when they are designing and making things, for if they are constantly prompted to observe aspects of the environment which surround them in producing source materials for development in creative activities, they will, indeed, become increasingly aware of the inexhaustible variety and complexity of the objects in the physical world – whether these are simple or more sophisticated.

Technological extensions to human sight, such as photomicrography, X-ray and time-lapse photography, help us to ensure that the children's boundaries of the visible world expand, not only to show them the external appearance of natural and fabricated phenomena but also the internal structure of materials – their cellular organization, growth patterns and even movement. Children find such aspects fascinating, but they may need to be reminded that although many such phenomena are invisible to their normal sight, they ar nevertheless 'real' and provide stimulating sources of reference for creative art, craft and design work while offering a continuing stimulus for children's natural curiosity.

The aesthetic qualities of the natural environment – for instance the harmony and variety of a stretch of landscape, the dynamic cycle of life which embraces decay and regeneration, the effects of weather upon natural material, etc., are potential sources of pleasure and interest and they provide a useful source of stimulus. The fabricated world, too, being part of the totality of the children's everyday surroundings, provides a source of imagery for creative work, and the physical products of technology, developed over the centuries, will give the children opportunities to study materials and the way these have been used in serving human needs. Children will have to handle materials when solving designing and making problems in order to understand the extent to which the nature of a material will affect the eventual outcome, and this can be combined quite logically with more historical and theoretical studies of design.

A group of top juniors tackled the idea of 'Aspects of the physical world' as a project. Theirs was a normal primary classroom with a limited range of materials and facilities. They were able to use paints,

131

crayons, adhesives, twine, and coloured pieces of felt and fabrics for collage work. The usual drawing materials were available.

The project started with a lively class discussion and this initiated some good ideas. The children focused for a time upon interesting cloud formations, sunsets and the effects of light and shadow. It revealed their interest in the beauty of spiders' webs covered with dew-drops, the patterns of pipes stacked neatly at the roadside, the shapes of shells, reflections in ponds and puddles of rain, pavement patterns and the shapes of trees.

The children discussed the importance of recognizing and appreciating such simple, everyday things and it was agreed that everyone is affected by objects which are to be discovered around us. One bright little girl made the observation that when people looked closely at things they widened their horizons and a different world was opened up to them.

The discussion then considered fabricated objects – ranging from bridges to dressmaker's pins – and it was interesting that the teacher noted that a similar attitude prevailed. Two of the children put forward ideas concerned with the shapes of buildings based upon natural forms (e.g. the use of spirals in shells). Another interesting point which was raised was – in simpler terms than here – that nature creates a certain harmony in her constructions and that these related to the environment in a purely functional, yet beautiful, way. Some of the children thought that the fabricated forms suffered from a conflict between harmony of form, functionalism and the environment, and examples given were 'the thoughtless building of houses without any consideration for the places in which they were', 'pylons stretching across beautiful areas of countryside', 'bad town planning', 'huge, ugly factory buildings', and so on. They did, however, see a certain beauty in cranes and tractors, smooth stainless steel door handles, exciting examples of architecture, church spires, fan tracery in churches – which looked liked trees, some pieces of machinery, and the inside of clocks.

Once they were discussing in an uninhibited way, some everyday objects were suggested for pattern-making. These included teapots, clocks, watches, small machine parts, scissors and other household objects. The children suddenly felt that such objects had potential for design and pattern-making and they began to make drawings.

It was decided that everyone in the class would go on looking when away from school, making notes and collecting some interesting objects. They said they would focus in on natural forms: the patchwork patterns made by fields; the erosion on hillsides; the stunted weirdness of trees against the sky; leaves; and the shadows of clouds on hills and valleys. As this school was situated in a small country village this was an easy thing to do. Many things were found and brought into class. They included, amongst other things, small insects, snails, frogs, lichen, beautiful pieces of bark, one old and battered saucepan, rusty tin, twigs, leaves and stones, and they were placed in a carefully labelled display for all to see.

Someone looked behind a piece of bark and discovered beetle tracks. This started a new interest in 'cutting things open and looking inside' rather than simply looking at the outside of objects. Some of the onions, tomatoes and other natural objects were cut up in different ways to reveal inside them patterns, colours and textures which could be drawn or copied with a brush and colour. One of the teachers brought in a microscope and a great deal of observation went on using onion skins, sections cut through the stems of flowers, flower stamens, petals and even dead insects. Magnifying glasses were also used and every pupil examined pieces of lichen found on tree bark with a new sense of wonder. They were amazed at the complex structures which the magnifying glass and microscope revealed – and although the classroom soon became a somewhat damp and smelly 'object dump' it fostered an eagerness to become involved in doing something.

Pupils did a lot of observational drawings. Some of these were very carefully conceived, small sketches in pen and ink, others were made with large brushes and paint. They produced rubbings of bark patterns and their surface textures. One pupil, fascinated by lichens, looked through the microscope, made a drawing and then blew this up to a large size before doing a number of copies in colour. It led her on to design a collage picture using small pieces of brightly coloured felt to make it look rich. Before doing the final picture she made paper patterns of the shapes and eventually made the felt collage by sticking the various shapes down on to strong hessian. She then added coloured beads, coloured threads and sequins.

A boy chose a knot in a piece of wood and took that as a starting point. After producing some drawings of it in pencil and colour washes, he then moved into pattern-making with coloured threads which were stuck down on to a firm base. Other children chose cellular structures which they found in science. The drawings, painted patterns, collages, embroideries and paintings which resulted contained abstract qualities, with the pupils selecting certain parts of their chosen objects then changing and stylizing them to suit what they had in mind. Many seemed to know immediately what they wanted to achieve and set to with paint and inks to fill in and add to their work; others chose restricted ranges of colour, working in tones of one or two colours which related closely to a chosen object. Some children worked with colours directly opposed to their objects and this tends to abstract their art work even more.

Several of the pupils became interested in using vegetables. They cut these across, split them open or hacked them into different shapes. A small group focused on tomatoes, looking at the cut shapes with magnifying glasses and making preliminary sketches in coloured crayons and paints. Following this stage they tended to diverge in what they produced, some going into simple textile printing and making multicoloured over-prints, others doing large painted designs, and others making wire and paper sculptures.

One boy became engrossed with a cauliflower. After making some drawings of it he then used beans and seeds, and designed a collage picture which he painted over with delicate colours. Later he used the cauliflower image to make a string print on which he did some over-printing and filling-in with coloured inks. The colours he used in his work were completely unrelated to natural colours but led him to produce some very exciting and refreshingly different ideas in visual form.

PVA and 'dribble paintings' were also engaged in by some children, but only two attempted to make constructions. This was disappointing for the teacher, especially as incidental discussions had suggested that more of them might be willing to work with three-dimensional materials.

A small number of the children took everyday objects used in the kitchen as starting points. These included items of cutlery and machine-made parts from some old clocks. They created patterns with these and then translated their ideas into coloured card.

Three pupils drew buildings. They then took small parts of these and enlarged them on large sheets of cartridge paper. This meant that they had to abstract their shapes and pattern elements so that the large mural which resulted was strong and effective. Two girls, interested in old cars, made copied drawings from a magazine on automobiles. From these drawings they made simple templates and drew around these to produce overlapping images in their patterns.

One group of four pupils were very interested in dockside cranes. They did drawings from photographs and then picked out certain shapes and went on to do overlapping patterns, paintings and prints in black, grey and silver.

In evaluating the material after a period of some three weeks, several observations and conclusions were reached:

- most of the pupils had had a lot of satisfaction in looking at environmental forms
- they had been fascinated by using natural and/or fabricated forms – especially by abstracting and stylizing them to their own needs
- some children had never considered using shadows to obtain effects in art work and those who did saw a lot of potential in this area
- cellular structures were revealed to them under microscopes and magnifying glasses and stimulated much more interest and potential ideas
- all manner of shapes, patterns and textures became apparent and stimulated the creation of new ones in materials
- every pupil felt that he or she had expanded their ideas and expertise as designers and artists
- some children felt that they would have liked to have looked more closely at 'decay' and 'regeneration', others at 'the effect of light and shadows'
- some wanted to consider 'movement' or 'structure of buildings'

In some respects the teacher felt that the project itself was much too broad in scope and that it would be better to have a more restricted idea in the future. In general, the class felt that they had been stimulated to look more carefully at their daily world with an increased sense of wonder and appreciation.

This class had been introduced to a 'normal' lesson theme which had, in fact, been taken beyond the normal boundaries by the sensitivity of the teacher, who was aware of the moments when she was needed or when she felt some instruction or direction was necessary and when they were not. She was aware that she sometimes tended to over-direct work or, on the other hand, to totally withdraw, expecting her pupils to discover qualities in their studies when they did not possess the skills or knowledge with which to tackle some problems. If, then, as teachers, we recognize such a dilemma, it can be related to particular children with particular problems and we can cater better for their educational needs.

Case study 2

One vital aspect of doing work in art, design and craft is that children have to think for themselves. I believe it was Jean-Jacques Rousseau who said, 'If we do not form the habit of thinking as children, we shall lose the power of thinking for the rest of our lives', and we must remember, therefore, to give the pupils in our charge opportunities for creative thinking when they are in school.

'Design' activities are fundamentally different from those which go on in art in that they are not aesthetically-centred but essentially problem-solving activities related to human needs and wants in which some technological means are used. As a curriculum aspect, design is an area of activity in which problems are invariably imposed while having external contraints such as 'fitness for purpose', 'function', and 'suitability of material or process' to contend with. The socially constructive and interdisciplinary nature of craft, in contrast to art, makes it an attractive counterpart to art in school, and helps children to realise product design and function better. An increased knowledge of it – possibly through some experience of doing it – will help children to become better educated and more discriminating consumers as adults.

The design aspect embraces, as noted already, problem-solving activities and it involves divergent and creative thinking, not simply a preoccupation with the production of objects. Design tasks provide excellent educational opportunities for problem-solving but we must set children a well-considered brief. Such a brief will, ideally, result in a variety of solutions which do not necessarily conform to those which we as teachers, might subconsciously have pre-determined ourselves, but which will often be unexpected, more realistic and exciting.

Whether we set definite problems for pupils to explore and solve, or allow them to identify a need for themselves and then strive for a solution to fulfil that need, children will effect solutions at their own level of intelligence, creativity, knowledge and manual competence. Their first need will be to exploit materials in order to come to terms with their varying properties and characteristics. With careful teacher control this can be done so that it will lead to problem-solving in which each pupil determines the materials he or she will use: knowledge based upon experience. Such work is likely to be self-evaluating since solutions can be tested in such a way that pupils can see the shortcomings and virtues of their own responses. It also provides opportunities for fruitful groupwork in which pupils gain a great deal from the exchange of ideas and discussion of criteria, methodologies and results.

The government is legislating for design and technology to be included in the primary curriculum from September 1990, so that children spend 10 per cent of their school lives designing, making, appraising and repairing things. At the age of eleven pupils of average ability will be expected to be able to:

- Use scissors to cut cardboard, a saw to cut wood, a computer keyboard to enter data;
- Use working sketches and diagrams;
- Suggest a possible solution to a problem which arises during making: for example, suggest different means of dealing with wheel spin in a vehicle they have designed;
- Compare and contrast what they have made with the original design intentions;
- Understand why, for example, the cardboard model worked well until tried in water;
- Incorporate aesthetic considerations;
- Discuss, write about and produce illustrated accounts of what they have designed and made;
- Show they understand the product's economic and social effects.

(DES, *Interim Report on Design & Technology in the National Curriculum*, produced by a working party under the chairmanship of Lady Parkes, published 24 November 1988)

So all primary teachers will be involved with this aspect whether they have had some training in it or not.

At one primary school in a large LEA children are already introduced to 'design and craft' work at an early age, when they are expected to engage in using both hand- and simple power tools. Teachers in the school feel that it is important that they not only adjust to these quickly, which they appear to do quite readily, but also maintain their initial enthusiasm so that it becomes a strong internal force leading them on to their own discovery learning.

In teaching aspects of introductory CDT, however, some teachers often feel the need to sacrifice 'design' and 'creative experience' so that children simply concentrate upon technique. But is it possible to bring these together while maintaining standards and interest. Work done by pupils in this particular school has revealed that children have an ability to design and to master techniques in producing good work.

The following is a brief account of an introductory course which attempts to set a child along a path of creative design by, at first, arousing the need to learn. Some direct teaching – possibly in the form of demonstrations – is included occasionally, but allows the pupils to develop their own practical expertise with stimulus being of an internal rather than a teacher-imposed form. The children are given up to three problems which they must attempt to solve. At first one or two simple problems are given so that the pupils can begin to understand the problem-solving, design situation, and then others are introduced as they become more competent. In this example 'wood' was the material used – although the same approach can be used with other materials and apparatus.

The task: design and make a 'soil-turning' implement

Materials/tools: Some lengths of wood, saws, cutting knives, glasspaper.

The design processes involved in this simple task are the same as those involved in the designing of an aeroplane, an office block, or a wooden crate. Ideas in sketch and note form must be made before the final solution to the problem is undertaken, to allow the young designer to think on paper. This helps him or others to tease out the problem, which can be understood better by noting some semi-structured techniques.

The problem given to the children was to use a piece of wood to design and make a hand-held tool with which an old person could turn over the soil in a window box. They needed to consider:

1 size
2 shape (would the tool be comfortable to hold? would it do the job?)

This meant that they had to think about the problems:

- what is the object for?
- what is its job to be?
- how big will it need to be?
- as wood is to be used, what shaping/making tools will be needed?
- what size and shape will this tool need to be?

Experiment

- make sketches on paper outlining your idea
- if possible, talk with one or two old people and discuss the problem with them
- make a preliminary model in cardboard (or other material)
- think about a 'good', aesthetically pleasing shape for the tool while remembering that it must be functional
- try out your preliminary model(s) to see if it(they) will do the job
- make notes – written and verbal – and modify your ideas

Keep all your materials in a folder –which will be your 'design job file' and which will contain your own critical comments.

During the initial 'designing' stage sketch ideas will evolve. This is a most important experimental and discovery stage during which the children must be given freedom, and certainly not told what to do. Their working drawings will enable the children to explain what they have in mind and how they are proceeding and these will be complemented by written comments and notes.

The teacher may, from time to time, need to demonstrate some skills and techniques as and when required and these will, most likely, be determined by the problems arising. The correct and skilful use of individual tools and materials must be emphasised simply in order to help the children to complete the problem.

Exploratory problems such as this one will embrace both successes and failures. Group discussions will be helpful as will analyses of the acheivements made at various stages. Children overcome disappointments quickly, and will be elated by success. It is a constructive way of working which is intended to encourage them to make further attempts which, it is hoped, will improve upon the achievements of the project.

Brief glossary of terms

Arrangement The composing of visual and tactile-related elements into pleasing composition, patterns, pictures, structures, etc.

Colour In artwork we depend upon the varying qualities of light evoked by different colours in producing works of art, which affect the emotions of the observer.

- *primary colours* – red, blue, yellow
- *secondary colours* – mixed primaries such as green, orange, violet, etc.
- *complimentaries* – red/green, blue/orange, yellow/violet, etc.

Form This term refers to shape manifested in three-dimensional objects, pots, sculptures, structures, etc.

Line Artists at the Bauhaus earlier this century defined line quite simply as an extended point, thick, thin, straight, curved.

Pattern Arrangements of shapes, lines, colours, textures, random or repeated.

Shape A two-dimensional area defined on a flat or raised surface.

Texture The quality we see (visual) or can feel (tactile) on a surface – roughness and smoothness.

Tone Lightness or darkness – usually applied to drawings, prints, paintings, etc.

Bibliography

Adams, E. and Ward, C. (1982) *Art and the Built Environment*, Harlow, Essex: Longman & Schools Council.

Adams, E. and Baynes, K. (1982) *Art and the Built Environment: Study Activities*, Harlow, Essex: Longman & Schools Council.

Allison, B. (1973) 'Sequential programming in art education', in D. W. Piper and Lund Davis, *Reading in Art Education*, London: Davis Poynter.

—— (1982) 'Identifying the core in art and design', *Journal of Art and Design Education* 1, 1: 55–6.

Bantock, G. H. (1963) *Education in an Industrial Society*, London: Faber.

Barnes, R. (1988) *Teaching Art to Young Children 4–9*, London: Unwin Hyman.

—— (1989) *Art, Design and Topic Work, 8–13*, London: Unwin Hyman.

Barret, M. (1979) *Art Education: A Strategy for Course Design*, London: Heinemann.

Bayliss, S. (1988) 'HMI foresees subject specialists', *Times Educational Supplement*, 7 October.

Baynes, K. (1976) *About Design*, London: Design Council.

Birmingham Education Department, City of (1980) *Further Developments in the Primary Curriculum: Art and Craft*, Birmingham: City of Birmingham Education Department.

Boden, T. (ed.) (1982) *Learning through Art in the Primary School*, Leicester: Leicestershire Education Committee.

Bristol School of Art Education, *Archives*, Bristol: Bristol Polytechnic/University of Bristol School of Education.

Brittain, W. L. (1978) *Creativity and the Young Child*, London: Collier Macmillan.

Brooke-Little, J. P. (1978) *Boutell's Heraldry*, London and New York: Warne.

—— (1981) *Royal Heraldry: Beasts and Badges of Britain*, Derby: Pilgrim Press.

Brough, L. (1985) *Design and Making*, Birmingham: East Midlands and Yorkshire Forum of Advisers in Craft, Design and Technology.

Buber, M. (1961) *Between Man and Man*, New York: Fontana.

Calouste Gulbenkian Foundation (1982) *The Arts in Schools: Principles, Practice and Provision*, London: Calouste Gulbenkian.

Carpi, P. (ed.) (1979) *The Book of Art*, London & Tonbridge: Ernest Benn Ltd.

Clement, R. (1986) *The Art Teacher's Handbook*, London: Hutchinson.

Curtis, A. M. (1966) *A Curriculum for the Pre-School Child: Learning to Learn*, Windsor: NFER–Nelson.

Crafts Council, *Crafts Magazine*, London: Crafts Council.

Dean, J. (1963) *Art and Crafts in the Primary School Today*, London: Black.

—— (1973) *Room to Learn: Display*, London: Evans.

—— (1975) *A Place to Paint*, London: Evans.

D.E.S. (1959) *Primary Education*, London: HMSO.

—— (1978a) *Art in Junior Education*, London: HMSO.

—— (1978b) *Primary Education in England: A Survey by HMI, HMSO*, London: HMSO.

—— (1981) *The School Curriculum*, London: HMSO.

—— (1985a) *Craft, Design and Technology in Schools: Some Successful Examples*, London: HMSO.

—— (1985b) *The Curriculum from 5–16 (Curriculum Matters 2)*, London: HMSO.

—— (1985c) *The School Curriculum* (seventh impression), Cardiff: HMSO Welsh Office.

—— (1987a) *Craft, Design and Technology from 5–16*, London: HMSO.

—— (1987b) *Primary Schools: Some Aspects of Good Practice*, London: HMSO.

—— (1989) *National Curriculum: From Policy to Practice*, London: HMSO.

—— (1989) *Design and Technology for Ages, 5–16*, London: HMSO.

Design Council Report (1987) *Design and Primary Education*, London: Design Council.

Dewey, J. (1958) *Art as Experience*, London: Putnam.

Dyke, W. (1842) *The Drawing Book of the School of Design*, London.

Eggleston, J. (ed.) *Studies in Design Education, Craft and Technology*, University of Warwick: Trentham Books.

Eisener, E. W. and Ecker, D. (1966) *Readings in Art Education*, Waltham, Massachusetts: Blaisdell.

Eisener, E. W. (1972) *Educating Artistic Vision*, New York: Macmillan.

—— (1985) *The Art of Educational Evaluation*, New York: Flamer Press.

East Midlands and Yorkshire Forum of Advisers in Craft, Design, Technology (1985) *Exhibition Catalogue: Designing and Making: Learning through Craft, Design, Technology*, Leeds.

Field, D. (1970) *Change in Art Education*, London: Routledge & Kegan Paul.

Field, D. and Newick, J. (eds) (1973) *The Study of Education and Art*, London: Routledge.

Figg, G. (1985) 'In search of a curriculum model for the primary schools', *Journal of Design and Education* 4, 1: 35–51.

Fox-Davies, A. (1985) *The Complete Guide to Heraldry*, London: Bloomsbury Books.

—— (1986) *The Art of Heraldry*, London: Bloomsbury Books.

—— (1988) *Heraldic Designs*, London: Bracken Books.

Friar, S. (1987) *A New Dictionary of Heraldry*, London: A. & C. Black.

Gentle, K. (1981) 'The development of children's art', *Education 3–13* 9, 2.

—— (1985) *Children and Art Teaching*, London: Croom Helm.

Grampian Region Council Education Department (1983) *A Guide to Art Education in Primary Schools*, Aberdeen: Grampian Region Council Education Department.

H.M. Government (1988) *Education Reform Act*, London: H.M. Government.

Hampshire Education Authority (1987) *Guidelines for Art Education from 5–18*, Winchester: Hampshire Education Authority.

Hoyland, M. (July 1971) 'Primary advice', *The Bulletin of the National Society for Art Education*, Corsham: NSAE.

Hooper, R. (ed.). (1971) *The Curriculum: Context, Design and Development*, Edinburgh: Oliver & Boyd in association with The Open University Press.

Inner London Education Authority (1981a) *Learning to Look*, London: ILEA Learning Materials Services.

—— (1981b) *Looking*, London: ILEA Learning Materials Services.

—— (1981c) *Starting*, London: ILEA Learning Materials Services.

Innes-Smith, R. (1980) *An Outline of Heraldry in England and Scotland*, Derby: Pilgrim Press.

Jameson, K. (1971) *Junior School Art*, London: Studio Vista.

—— (1973) *Pre-School and Infant Art*, London: Studio Vista.

Kellog, R. (1955) *What Children Scribble and Why*, San Francisco: National Press.

—— (1970) *Analysing Children's Art*, San Francisco: National Press.

Lancaster, Janet and Gaunt, J. (1976) *Developments in Early Childhood Education*, London: Open Books.

Lancaster, J. (1969) 'Visual education in schools and colleges', *Studies in Education and Craft* 1, 2: 12–15.

—— (1971a) 'The artist looks at the school environment' *Froebel Journal*, London; 19: 12–14.

—— (1971b) 'Integrated work in schools: with particular reference to the role of art' *International Journal of Education Sciences* 4,3: 129–34.

—— (1971c) 'The pattern of the integrated day', *International Journal of Education Science* 4, 3: 135–7.

—— (1973) 'An integrated art workshop curriculum innovation: art in a professional course of teacher education', *Studies in Design Education and Craft* 6, 1: 5–30.

—— (1974) 'Art education and the importance of materials', *Studies in Art Education (NAEA): A Journal of Issues and Research in Art Education*, 15, 3: 40–3.

—— (1978) 'Art in primary teacher education: a comparative study of an integrated and a non-integrated professional studies course', unpublished M.Phil. thesis, University of London.

—— (1985) 'An historical study of specialist art teacher education in Bristol', unpublished Ph.D. thesis, University of London.

Lancaster, J. (ed.) (1987) *Art, Craft and Design in the Primary School* (second edition), Corsham: National Society for Education in Art and Design.

Lancaster, J. (1988a) *Card*, London: Franklin Watts.

—— (1988b) *Paper*, London: Franklin Watts.

Langer, S. (1957) *Problems of Art*, London: Routledge & Kegan Paul

—— (1958) *Reflections of Art*, Baltimore: Johns Hopkins.

—— (1963) *Feeling and Form*, London: Routledge & Kegan Paul.

Leeds Education Authority (undated) *Art and Design Education in Leeds*, Leeds: Leeds Education Authority.

Lowenfeld, V. (1963) *Your Child and his Art*, New York: Macmillan.

—— (1964) *Creative and Mental Growth*, London: Macmillan.

Lowenfeld, V. G. and Brittain, W. L. (1982) *Creative and Mental Growth*, New York: Macmillan.

MacDonald, S. (1970) *The History and Philosophy of Art Education*, London: UCP.

MacGregor, R. N. (1977) *Art Plus*, Toronto: McGraw-Hill Ryerson Ltd.

Manchester Education Committee (undated) *The Looking and Touching, Asking and Learning for Drawing and Painting Book*, Manchester: Manchester Education Committee.

Metzi, K. (1967) *Art in the Primary School*, Oxford: Basil Blackwell.

Mid Glamorgan Education Committee (1984) *An Approach to Art in the Primary School*, Glamorgan: Mid Glamorgan Education Committee.

Morley, J. (1983) *Child Art Revolution 1930–1960*, London: Festival Hall.

Neubecker, (1976) *Heraldry Sources, Symbol and Meaning*, Maidenhead: McGraw-Hill.

Newick, S. (1973) 'A study of the context of participation in the Arts', in Field, D. and Newick, S. (eds) *The Story of Education and Art*, London: Routledge & Kegan Paul.

Open University (1987) 'A continuing education course', *Curriculum in Action: An Approach to Evaluation*, Milton Keynes: Open University Press.

Parry, M. (1980) *Early Years: Painting and Drawing*, Bristol: Bristol Education Committee.

Piaget, J. (1926) *Language and Thought of the Child*, London: Routledge & Kegan Paul.

Pickering, J. M. (1971) *Visual Education in the Primary School*, London: Batsford.

Potter, N. (1980) *What is a Designer: Education and Practice, a Guide for Students and Teachers*, London: Studio Vista.

Read, H. (1942) *The Meaning of Art*, London: Faber.

—— (1958) *Education through Art*, London: Faber.

Richardson, M. (1948) *Art and the Child*, London: University of London Press.

Ritson, J. E. and Smith, J. A. *Creative Teaching of Art in the Elementary School*, Boston, London, Sydney: Allen and Unwin.

Robertson, S. (1963) *Creative Crafts in Education*, London: Routledge & Kegan Paul.

Rosewell, G. (1983) *Teaching Art in Primary Schools*, London: Evans.

Scheffer, I. (1966) *Philosophy and Education*, New York: Allan & Bacon Incorporated.

Schools Council (1969) *Working Paper 26: Education through the use of Materials*, London: Evans.

—— (1974a) *Children's Growth through Creative Experience: Art and Craft Education 8–13*, London: van Nostrand Reinhold.

—— (1974b) *Design for Today*, London: Arnold.

—— (1974c) *Materials and Design*, London: Arnold.

—— (1975) *Education through Design and Craft*, London: Arnold.

—— (1978) *Art 7–11*, London: Schools Council.

—— (1981) *Resources for Visual Education 7–13*, London: Schools Council.

—— (1983) *Working paper 75: Primary Practice*, London: Methuen.

Sharples, D. E. (1985) 'Three-dimensional work in the primary school', *Journal of Art and Design Education* 4, 1: 53–60.

Skilbeck, M. (1970) *Dewey*, London: Collier Macmillan.

Storry, J. G. (1986) *Church Heraldry*: Nettlebed.

Suffolk County Council (1985) *Art 4–11*: Suffolk & Berol.

Sutton, G. (1967) *Artist or Artisan? A History of the teaching of Art and Crafts in English Schools*, Oxford: Pergamon Press.

Taylor, R. (1986) *Education for Art: Critical Response and Development*, London: Longman.

Thistlewood, D. (ed.) (1989) *Critical Studies in Art and Design Education*, Harlow, Essex: Longman.

Tomlinson, R. R. (1944) *Children as Artists*, London: Penguin.

Viola, W. (1942) *Child Art*, London: University of London Press.

Walters, E. H. (1968) *Activity and Experience in the Infant School*, London: National Froebel Foundation.

Woodcock, T. and Robinson, J. M. (1988) *The Oxford Guide to Heraldry*. Oxford: Oxford University Press.

Woof, T. (1976) *Developments in Art Teaching*, London: Open Books.

Ziegfeld, E. (ed.) (1953) *Educating Art*, UNESCO.

Index

147

Index